A Seasonal life

Tales of a Jersey Hotelier

— With every good wish

Graham.

22 Oct 2021.

By
Graham Anderson

All artwork by Lorand Sipos.

Shield Crest

ISBN: 978-1-913839-21-5

MMXXI

A CIP catalogue record for this book
is available from the British Library

Published by
ShieldCrest Publishing Ltd.,
Aylesbury, Buckinghamshire,
HP18 0TF England
Tel: +44 (0) 333 8000 890
www.shieldcrest.co.uk

To my late parents who sent me to France, where I learned to appreciate the language, the culture and above all the gastronomy of the country.

To my four sons, their late mother, Sandra and to Philip, my eldest who has successfully carried on with running the hotel, along with his wife, Christine.

To all the staff, past and present and in particular to John and Pauline Dryhurst and Sue Robson, who have worked tirelessly alongside me and contributed so much through their hard work, kindness and dedication to the success of our family enterprise. Also a big "thank you" to my Barbara.

Our full brigade at 'La Bourride'.

Growing Up in London & Essex

At the time, it was not considered to be the most desirable place where one would want to be born, but that is where it happened. My parents had a baker's shop in Watney Street in Stepney, East London, and as usual, my mother was helping my father with moulding the dough. This was before they could afford the luxury of machinery to produce the dough that was subsequently turned into the crusty bread that made them famous in that part of London. As my mother would repeat many times later: "I was helping Tom in the bakery and I was taken short" - meaning that my birth was not only imminent but was actually happening at that moment, so she had to down tools and go upstairs above the shop with the nurse and then give birth to me. Born within the sound of Bow Bells, that officially makes me a cockney. Actor Terence Stamp was also born in Stepney, as were EastEnders actress Anita Dobson and authors Alan Yentob, Arnold Wesker and singer Kenny Lynch, so I am in varied and illustrious company.

Just a few streets away from Watney St was the notorious Cable St where a demonstration took place in 1936, led by the British Union of Fascists leader, Sir Oswald Mosley. This led to clashes between three dimensions: the anti-fascist supporters, Oswald Mosley and the police. Many years before this event, there occurred a siege in Sidney Street in 1911 when Winston Churchill, as Home Secretary, personally took charge of a dangerous situation when a group of Eastern European political dissidents and anarchists took control of premises in that particular street. Police and firemen suffered injuries, which resulted in several deaths.

Stepney, being an economically deprived area of East London, had a very left-wing anti-fascist community, and this was evident when an anti-fascist named Philip Piratin – sponsored by the Communist Party in 1945 – was one of the very few communists ever elected to Parliament in 1945. Again, all this within a stone's throw of my birthplace. This part of East London also had the highest number of Jewish immigrants in the UK.

As a family, we did not live in Stepney but had a small family home in Woodford Green which backed directly on to Epping Forest. I was the youngest; my sister Kitty was the eldest, then came Derek, and after him, there was Alan. I was told that I was an extremely quiet child, but I was a very good listener, and around the table in the kitchen where as a family we used to sit, the conversation was invariably concerning the bakery and whatever problems there were, either concerning the day-to-day functioning of the business or problems with the staff. It was an atmosphere of discipline, respect, work ethic and a certain pride in being independent of officialdom or government. Matters of social security and benefits from the State were, I felt, an anathema, particularly to my father. My mother was perhaps more pragmatic and realistic and more liberal than Dad. They were, however, wonderful parents, and despite the slight difference in their respective characters, they gave us all an excellent start in life and encouraged us in whichever career or direction we chose to follow. The idea of success was constantly instilled in us, and I do feel that we have all been affected by this urge to do better and to find the formula that would make us independent and financially secure. My parents did have another son Tommy who unfortunately died prematurely after a fall at school in the playground. He died from septicaemia. This was some years before the invention of penicillin. Mum spoke about him so often that I felt that I should feel closer to him than I did but try as hard as I could to feel brotherly love for him, it was more a feeling of sympathy for my mother, who would often shed tears over him. I have often asked myself if it was some juvenile form of jealousy, but as I never knew him and was born so many years after his death, I dismissed this as a phenomenon with no connection to my being jealous of him.

Something I never understood was Dad's desire and discouragement that Alan or I should not make a career in the bakery business. Derek, being the eldest son, automatically fitted in with Dad's desire to have the moral and practical support that he was looking for. Perhaps the reason for Alan and me not having this incentive was, I think, because Dad left school at a very early age and wanted to give us an education and an opportunity that he never had. However, this worked out well in the end because Derek gave Dad the support he needed at just the right time. My sister went on to help manage the La Ronde restaurant in Loughton with a friend. Alan received top grades at school and went on to achieve a degree with honours at Oxford University while I was still at school in London. Alan subsequently qualified as a solicitor and set up a successful practice in Loughton, Essex.

It was a very poor exam result in French that was to be the catalyst for an advantageous change in my life, not only at that time but for the future of a young, immature fourteen-year-old. My end of term exam results were lying on the breakfast table, and as I entered, I observed the expression on my parents' respective faces that showed a discontent that would be made known to me as soon as I tucked into my breakfast.

Dad said, "You have come seventeenth out of twenty-four fellow pupils. That is not good enough. Your mother and I have decided to send you to France for a month, and you will stay with a French family whom Mrs Rooney will recommend". Mrs Rooney, despite her surname, was a French national who had been married to an Irishman. She had already given French lessons to Alan and Kitty, and now it was my turn, so after half a dozen lessons with her, she promptly informed my parents that she had found a French family with a similar request. Their son Jacques would spend a month with us in Woodford, and then together, we would return to Brive for a further month with his family. Jacques, like me, was fourteen years old and on his own made his way from Brive to Calais on the train and then he took the ferry on to Dover. He eventually arrived at our house along with Mrs Rooney, who introduced him to us all. He seemed very distant, perhaps shy, and he was not quite what I expected him to be. I had already been abroad with my family to France and had noticed that our typical English reserve and shyness were almost as conspicuous as the ebullient and charming ways of Latin people, who used their hands a great deal when speaking and kissed each other a lot on the cheek, something I had never seen in England.

At the time, I thought that Jacques was the very opposite of what I remembered of French people. He was distant and unwilling to learn English even though Mrs Rooney's task was to give him English lessons three times a week. He made little progress and remained silent and aloof. He did not seem to be enjoying his stay with us. In his defence, I suppose his coming to a foreign country for the first time may have been a challenge for him. I think what upset me most was his attitude to English food. My mother, when not working in the bakery, was always in the kitchen, and whenever I came home with any school friends, she always had a routine regarding food and her capacity in making everyone feel welcome. She would seat us around the kitchen table, put on the pepper and salt, mustard and tomato ketchup and then, as if by magic, she would produce several plates of eggs, bacon, sausages, mushrooms and tomatoes, and several pots of tea. In fact, it was only tea at that time as I could never ever remember drinking coffee. If anyone came to the house, the stock phrase would be, "I'll put the kettle on and make a nice cup of tea." That meant warming not only the china pot but the individual cups as well. When in later years instant coffee became available, Mum would make it with a hundred per cent boiled milk and lots of sugar. On one such occasion, I was served this mixture, and Mum must have forgotten to put in the sugar. It was that enjoyable that since that day, I have never taken sugar in any beverage. However, Jacques had other ideas regarding the culinary shortcomings in our household. He refused to drink tea, and I believe that was the moment I tasted coffee for the first time. However, at the time, coffee meant a dark liquid treacly substance called 'Camp Coffee', which Jacques disliked intensely. I must be honest and say that I agreed totally with him on this point. It was really a liquid, black in colour and sweet with molasses and a taste that had nothing in common with real coffee.

Jacques then informed me that ketchup would never be tolerated on his parents' table, along with Colman's mustard and other such things. He then went on to criticise our food and mentioned that where he came from, there were delicacies such as *foie gras* and truffles – food I had never heard of, and neither had my parents. He attended classes regularly with Mrs Rooney, but either he did not wish to speak to us or endeavour to practise our language, so we accepted the fact that he was morose and perhaps, this being his first trip away from his own environment, he was missing his family.

The weeks passed, and finally, it was time to pack my little suitcase and leave England along with Jacques. Dad drove us to Euston Station and from there, we both got on the train that was to take us to Dover. I was very excited because even though I had looked at a map of France, I did not know exactly where I would be going. Deep into the Corrèze region, it was a place I had never even visited with my parents before. Jacques was still very quiet and hardly spoke. I behaved in the same jovial way as usual, but he was even less talkative than before. I thought I would play him at his own game, so conversation-wise, I pulled down the shutters. I only spoke to him when it was really necessary, such as the moment we had to show our passports on arrival at Dover and later in Calais. Mum had made us some cheese sandwiches with Branston pickle for our journey. I think Jacques must have been hungry because he ate his two rounds without his usual comment. It either meant that he enjoyed them or that he was so desperately hungry that he would literally eat anything.

Visiting France

We arrived in Calais and made our way to the train station, where we had to wait half an hour for the train that would take us to our destination: Brive. It was such a long time ago that I have forgotten where we had to change trains. I think it was in Angoulême, and from there, it was a straight run to our destination. What I remember most about both train journeys was the constant smell of garlic mixed with the fumes of Gauloise or Gitane cigarettes not just in each carriage but also along all the corridors. In one carriage, a man, his wife and two children were eating cold snacks from a portable wooden hamper, and from time to time, he would take a swig of red wine from a bottle that he had concealed somewhere amongst the crusty baguettes and *'pains à chocolat'*. I have always associated this mixture of garlic and tobacco with French trains, and even though this combination is no longer permissible with our modern political correctness regarding smoking in enclosed places, it is one disappearing feature of the past that I selfishly regret. I dislike smoking intensely, but the smell of Gitane tobacco is something I miss.

The train pulled into Brive Station, and as we got off with our luggage through the exit door, I could see an attractive lady and a gentleman waving ferociously at us. I assumed they were Jacques' parents. Monsieur Mazet was small in height, and I noticed an air of calm about him. They both shook my hand and led Jacques and me to a parked Maigret-type black light 16 Citroen. I was surprised to see Madame Mazet open the door to the driver's side and very neatly slide into the bucket seat. Monsieur Mazet sat in front next to his wife, and Jacques and I sat in the back. There was not a great deal of conversation, so I thought I would break the ice and practise my schoolboy French.

"Je suis très heureux d'être en France, Monsieur et Madame Mazet et enchanté de faire votre connaissance," I said.

Monsieur Mazet clapped three times and said in French that he was very impressed with my one-liner. Madame drove very fast, so I was glad she did not consider clapping at the wheel in harmony with her husband.

I had no idea what Jacques' parents did for a living or where I would be housed for the next month. It was not long before the car pulled up opposite a church and was carefully parked by the side of an optician's shop. The town seemed neat, tidy, prosperous and very peaceful. Well, it was night-time so I reckoned that when all the various shops opened the next day, I would see a vast difference in my new surroundings. So, Jacques' father was the main optician in Brive with a modern shop right in the town centre. This reminded me of my own father's philosophy when he would constantly repeat to my mother, "Kitty, if we are going to have a shop, it is position and passing trade that counts."

As the shop was closed, we pulled our cases out of the car and approached a small side door that Monsieur Mazet opened with a key attached to a massive bunch of other keys. The Mazets led me upstairs and introduced me to Rosette, who was a live-in housekeeper-cum-cook. We shook, hands and I mumbled, *"Enchanté."* She then showed me to my little room, which faced the church, and which was to be my home for the next month.

I was hungry, so when Monsieur Mazet said, *"Tu as faim, Graham,"* I replied that I was starving and ready to eat. He showed me to a nicely laid table with cold plates already in position and cloth napkins for four people. Then came my first big surprise. Whenever I had an evening meal with my family in Woodford, it was always served very hot, the meat slightly overcooked and accompanied always with a thick brown gravy—and Dad would always insist on hot plates for hot food. However, the table setting was perfect and neatly arranged with a beautiful tablecloth and matching napkins, but the one thing missing was the heat and cooking smells emanating from the kitchen. This was my first lesson in France. As I sat down with the family, I noticed that all the food in front of me was cold. However, it looked very tasty, and I was ravenous. I helped myself to *pâté*, ham, olives and cornichons and I did not feel too self-conscious at all about breaking a knob off the end of the baguette and dipping it into the home-made mayonnaise. This was the first time I had ever tasted real mayonnaise and it was Rosette who taught me how to make it: Separate the egg yolk from the white, add Dijon mustard to the yolk, whisk to emulsify and slowly add the vegetable oil until it thickens to a firm consistency and at the last moment, add a squeeze of lemon juice and a dash of white wine vinegar, shavings from a small clove of garlic and finally pepper and salt. I do believe that this introduction into this mayonnaise recipe was perhaps the very moment that would change my life for ever and direct me to a career that I would have missed out on had my parents not sent me to France. I used to look with fascination at the food that came out of that very small kitchen, and there was an aroma that I had never smelt before. We ate every day at one o'clock, and whether it was meat or fish, it was served hot—invariably on cold plates. What was left over from lunch turned up in some form of salad with a vinaigrette dressing in the evening. Rosette always used just a little red or white wine in the stock reduction, and sometimes she would add shallots with Madeira. One day I actually saw what a truffle looked like and found it hard to believe that such a puny and strangely shaped object could be so expensive and yet so tasty. My first encounter with truffles came one day in the form of an *omelette aux truffes*. To this day, I feel that, for me, to get the best out of a truffle, it has to be served in an omelette.

The day of my arrival went well. My accommodation was extremely comfortable. I got on well with Jacques' parents and got to know the housekeeper, Rosette. The church bells rang out at regular intervals, and Brive seemed to be a prosperous provincial town known for its gastronomy and a very different and pronounced regional French accent. However, what happened next shocked me. I awoke the next morning and heard Madame Mazet knocking at my door.

"Puis-je entrer?" she shouted.

"Yes, of course, Madame, please come in," I replied in French. She came in with a tray laden with food I had never seen before. The three slices of toast were cold, but I later discovered that these were called *'biscottes'* which could be bought in a packet. There was also the home-made damson jam to spread on these *biscottes*. The smell of real coffee was something I had never experienced before, and it was not served in a cup with a handle but was poured into a soup bowl with two small handles on either side. Compared to the Camp coffee I had tried at home, I felt that I was in another world. I was about to pick up my 'soup' bowl of coffee with both hands when Madame Mazet said, *"Jacques est parti à Bordeaux avec ses copins et son vélo."*

I asked her why he had left the day after our arrival, along with his racing bike, to join his friends in Bordeaux. I was angry because I had given him so much hospitality in Woodford, that this news came as a real shock to me. She gave a typically Gallic shrug of the shoulders and said, *"C'est comme ça."*

It was something I found hard to digest, and because of this selfish action on his part, it was something I would neither forget nor forgive until many years later. But more of this later.

I realised that my hosts were saddened by Jacques' decision to disappear with his friends to Bordeaux, but his departure was so sudden that not only did he not bother to say goodbye to me but I felt that this must have been a pre-arranged trip because he just would not have had enough time to make the necessary preparations for a month's absence from home in just one day.

Madame Mazet was aware that I would not have anyone of a similar age with whom I could be friends, so they very kindly contacted a widow who ran the local bakery and who had a son called Jean-Claude. I must say that he was polite, caring and kept me company during my month-long stay in Brive. Some years later, he would visit me in Woodford and stay with my family for just a week.

His brief visit was remembered by us all as he asked me to take him to a Catholic church for Sunday Mass.

The service went on as usual for about an hour or more. After half an hour, Jean-Claude got up and said that in France, such a service would not last that long. He left while a church packed with worshippers turned around and looked at him in disgust. When eventually the service finished, I went to look for him, and a parishioner who had left before me said that my friend who left church prematurely was having a pint in the Travellers' Friend, a nice cosy pub opposite the church. At the time, I found his leaving the church an embarrassment but the more I saw of French behaviour, which at the time seemed discourteous, the more I liked their frankness and unpredictability. Over the years, especially in restaurants, I noticed that if something was not quite as it should be, then they would make it known in no uncertain terms to the management, whereas an English person when asked if they enjoyed a meal, even though it was not cooked well or the service was bad, would reply, "Yes that was very nice, thank you" and complain later to their friends.

Jean-Claude also arranged for me to have a *'vélo'*—a little low-horsepower bike with a minuscule motor and together we would weave through the traffic in Brive and invariably finish up at the local swimming pool or go further afield and have a picnic that his mother had kindly prepared. Later that afternoon, I returned home on my bike and parked it in a little recess near the back door. As I was about to enter, Monsieur Mazet said he would like to introduce me to members of his staff. They all had a go at speaking English to me, but it was not a very successful effort. However, it was a pleasant meeting, and every time I saw Janine, the shop assistant or Monsieur Veidy, the optical technician, I taught them both a new word in English. As they were locking up the shop with a heavy metal door, I heard the English language being spoken outside on the pavement, but with a different accent. I shouted out, "Hello do you speak English?" and suddenly, through the metal door, they introduced themselves by saying that they were two American girls from New York and were "doing Europe and thought they would pop in and see France." I suppose that as no one in the Mazet household spoke any English this moment was for me, as a very young man abroad and alone for the first time in his life, a moment of happiness just hearing someone speaking my language.

It was only after I returned to England that I realised that this isolation from my native tongue was a blessing in disguise, so now every time young people seek my advice relating to learning French, I always advise them to stay with a French family where no one speaks a word of English, and also to avoid the temptation of seeking compatriots when abroad. This is one reason, on looking back, that Jacques' departure was a fortuitous advantage for me because I was not obliged to speak to him or his family in English, which was part of the original arrangement I had with him. I started to read *Le Monde* newspaper which I found very useful in finding out what was going on in the world. I had my little Collins dictionary constantly with me, which was a great source of linguistic guidance when I was unable to find *'le mot juste'*, especially when I was with friends of Monsieur Mazet and other people I wanted to impress.

One day, Monsieur Mazet asked me if I would like to accompany Madame Mazet, Rosette, and himself to an outdoor theatre to see a Shakespeare play in French. I said that I would like that very much, so the next day we all piled into the Citroen and half an hour later we arrived at a parking area just next to an open-air theatre. I remember from school days that I invariably found Shakespeare somewhat difficult to understand, but at fourteen years of age and in France with *Macbeth* about to be re-enacted in a foreign language, I thought this could be a memorable evening. After the performance, I told Monsieur Mazet that I was grateful to have witnessed Shakespeare in French and how much I genuinely enjoyed the evening. Then the family invited me for a *'digestif'* in a local bar. There was a group of very young people at a nearby table making a hell of a noise. I could see that most of the wine bottles on the table had taken a good hiding, and even though I was only fourteen, I have never liked a situation that could get out of hand. I also felt very protective towards Monsieur Mazet. Even though at my tender age I was not very tall, Monsieur Mazet was even smaller than me, and there was a particularly tall, fair-headed man who was waving his arms around and screaming the cursory French phrase, *"putain de merde"*, which is offensive, especially with women present. Fortunately, nothing of a serious nature ensued, so thankfully, we returned home as a family would after an evening out. More and more, I felt closer and totally at ease with my hosts because I felt that they treated me more like a son rather than an exchange student from a distant land. I do not know how they would have treated Jacques simply because he was not there for me to make the comparison.

I appreciate that nowadays it is quite normal for people to dine out once or twice or even more a week, but when I was young, I can only remember eating out with my parents and brother Alan once. I know the restaurant was Italian and that it was in Ilford in Essex, just a few miles from Woodford. My father was a prolific meat eater and ordered *'Tournedos Rossini'* for himself. He assumed that it would be a plainly served fillet steak. Of course, when it arrived in front of him, he did not expect to see *foie gras*, truffles, Madeira sauce and all the trimmings that quite correctly go with it.

"I didn't ask for this—I ordered a fillet steak!" The waiter took Dad's plate away and several minutes later returned with just the fillet steak, a little sauce and no trimmings. For some unknown reason, this event with Dad's fillet steak occurred to me when one day, Monsieur Mazet asked me if I would like to go out for a meal. I said I would love to. He said it was a special birthday of one of his employees, Monsieur Veidy. As usual, Madame Mazet drove the black Citroen to our destination. In fact, I had never been driven by a woman driver before. I knew that Monsieur Mazet could drive, but I think she did enjoy being in charge of any given situation. We arrived at a very grand and spectacular Château with beautiful wrought-iron gates that were opened by a uniformed member of staff. I was immediately aware of the potential expense of such an outing and felt quite humble and embarrassed at accepting my hosts' generosity.

What is so agreeable with the French is their warmth in greeting each other. I had never in my life seen people kissing on the cheek so often. The man who owned the Château clearly knew my hosts because he automatically went forward to kiss Madame Mazet on both cheeks, and lo and behold, he did the same to Monsieur Mazet. I was at first a little shocked, but it was something I not only got used to but thoroughly approved of—this blatant demonstration of affection. Around the table, which was long and oval, were seated twelve people, all of whom seemed to me to be of a certain age, except for one person who sat opposite me and who was a dark-haired girl with tanned skin and very young, perhaps about seventeen years of age. From time to time, she would smile at me and I would politely return her smile. We had something in common because we were the youngest people there. It just seemed that no one was speaking to her even though on either side of her, there were people I assumed she must have known. The men were discussing politics. I remember the men sounding quite menacing with what seemed to me to be raised voices when someone mentioned the names of Charles de Gaulle and René Coty.

When the menu arrived, I had a plan to improve my French. I would look at the menu and deliberately choose something whose title I did not understand in English, so if I liked what I had chosen, I would remember it for another time; if I did not like it, I would give it a wide berth in future. This method would build up my vocabulary. Then, something strange happened regarding the young girl opposite me. The waiter put down her starter in front of her, and suddenly the two of them started speaking to each other but not in French. She must have recognised the fact that he was Spanish when she heard him speaking French with a typically Spanish accent. The more they spoke—and the conversation must have

13

gone on for several minutes, the more the rest of the people around the table fell silent. Everybody was suddenly interested in this inconspicuous young teenager, who a few moments earlier was of no interest to anyone. Suddenly she was the centre of attention. Everybody wanted to know how or why she was so fluent in Spanish, and from this insignificant experience, I learned two important things, the first being that the knowledge of any language is of the utmost importance and secondly that it creates conversation and is a method of impressing people. Towards the end of the evening, she offered me a wry smile of satisfaction as if to say she had made her point and had impressed everyone around the table.

Monsieur Mazet also had a branch of his optician's business in the historic town of Sarlat, which he visited twice a week to carry out optical examinations on people who could not travel the distance to Brive. I went with him on these occasions, and it gave me the opportunity of visiting this beautiful 14th-century town, which is situated in what is known as 'Le Périgord Vert' with its cobbled streets and fascinating architecture.

My month in Brive was nearly up. It seemed to pass so quickly. I can honestly say that it was an experience spent with the kindest of people and was one of the happiest four weeks of my life. There was still one more surprise they had in store for me. I had never heard of the American singer and actress Josephine Baker before— after all, I was only fourteen years of age and knew nothing about American gospel music or politics. She was a Civil Rights activist, actress and singer whose politics were not accepted by the American Government at the time. Her expulsion from America came to a head when she was about to give a concert in the Deep South, and because of the stringent race laws at the time, she had to be confined to accommodation reserved strictly for black people. She had tried to stay in a luxury hotel where white people stayed, but she was immediately forced to stay in alternative lodgings reserved for black people only. This forced her to make a decision, so she decided not to return to America and thus found solace in France and spent time in Paris singing in cabaret. After leaving Paris, she decided to help and adopt underprivileged children from all backgrounds and cultures. She was a person of benevolent and universal qualities. This is where I was introduced to her. She had moved from Paris and had bought the beautiful Château des Milandes in Castelnaud-la-Chapelle. I could see that the Château was both remarkable and beautiful in its architecture and historical importance. It was built in the 15th century by François de Caumont for his wife. Suddenly, a very beautiful lady approached us; she was holding the hands of two Asiatic children and alongside were children of African origin running behind her. She recognised Monsieur Mazet, and because I was with them, she automatically bent down to plant two kisses on both my cheeks—a very Parisian gesture and not just the little one peck on the cheek you might receive outside of Paris. She did the same to Monsieur and Madame Mazet. It was not until many years later that I realised the importance of this meeting when I read about her struggle for equality and respect in America. Because she was rejected and later banned from entering her own country, she decided to move to France and dedicate her time and money to helping and housing underprivileged children from every culture in the world. She lived in her Château until her death in 1975. Because she refused to perform her songs in front of segregated audiences in America, she was to spend her final days in the country she came to love and a place she could finally call home. She also played a part in the Resistance movement and was praised by Général de Gaulle for her courage.

The day before my departure for home, I started to pack my small suitcase and looked for the small envelope containing francs that my mother gave me to buy Madame Mazet a beautiful bouquet of flowers to thank her for her hospitality. Mum was a very thoughtful lady with gestures such as this that made her so special. I went to the florist and ordered a bouquet of beautiful flowers. I made sure to secretly go to my room through the back entrance while Madame Mazet was at the hairdressers'. Once in my room, I consulted my Collins dictionary because I wanted to put something appropriate on my card to show my appreciation. I had never kissed Madame Mazet on the cheek before, but I thought that this would be the correct moment to do just that. I looked up the word for 'kiss' in my dictionary and found the word *'baiser'*. I felt that I was fluent enough for the next procedure. For anyone about to learn French, let this be a warning. It is often said by linguists that a dictionary can be a false friend. So meticulously, I set about saying in French, "Thank you, Madame Mazet, for your hospitality. I wish to thank you, and if I may, I am going to kiss you." *"Je vous remercie de votre gentillesse et hospitalité et si je peux je voudrais bien vous baiser."*

"Quoi?" she replied in astonishment and jokingly said in French, "I think you are a bit too young for that," with a wry look on her face. "No," she went on, *"'baiser'* used as a noun is perfectly correct, meaning a kiss but used as a verb, it means something very physical and personal that you would not appreciate at your age."

I apologised, blushed and this was a lesson that I have never forgotten. How easy for a beginner in French to commit such an error.

With my suitcase packed, I went downstairs to say goodbye to Monsieur Mazet's employees and promised to keep in touch with them, which I did for many years. I gave Rosette and Madame Mazet *'un bisou'* on the cheek and went with Monsieur Mazet in his car to Brive station. Just as the train arrived, he gave me a hug and a kiss, and I thanked him profusely for all his kindness. I opened the carriage door which suddenly gave way to the usual mixture of garlic and Gauloises.

"Don't open this now. Save it for later," he said as he put into my hand a small package wrapped in brown paper. We actually both cried. I leaned out of the window and waved until he was out of sight. On the train, I opened the package. What a surprise. It was a small book of published poetry written by him—Augustin Mazet.

On the train I spent most of my time standing in the corridor as the compartments were full to capacity—very hot with people eating snacks while others were snoring. I had to go to the toilet for a few moments and while I was washing my hands, I saw my reflection in the mirror. For me there has always been something attractive and exciting about the French, in the manner in which they dress and the dramatic hand movements that accompany their speech and just a month in Brive only served to strengthen that view. While I was there in Brive, I bought a grey sports jacket and a cheap pair of tinted glasses. They were so cheap I dared not show them to Monsieur Mazet, as his shop only dealt in branded and sophisticated frames. Now looking in the toilet mirror, I could see a difference in my appearance and demeanour, and I was pleased with what I saw. It pleased me even more when I returned to my place in the corridor and a rosy-cheeked man with, this time a Gitane cigarette in the corner of his mouth and looking for a light said, *"Vous avez du feu?"* At last someone thought I was French!

On the long journey home, I started chatting to a family from Normandy who complimented me on my French and it was not until then that I realised that I had made considerable progress and gained the confidence necessary to hold a conversation in French without resorting to the odd glimpse into my dictionary. Even though I was only fourteen, I decided that at a later stage in my life, I would buy a house in France with that particular region of Corrèze as a priority. As it turned out many years later it was not to be that region of France but more of that later.

My father was there to meet me at Victoria station in his Austin, A40. I was pleased to see him, naturally but I felt different, perhaps more mature than the young man I was when I left. Dad's car pulled up into the drive in Mornington Rd and the whole family was there waiting for me. "Where did you get that jacket from?" my sister Kitty asked "and what about your tinted glasses? And on top of that you have caught the sun." She went on, "You look more like a foreigner than an Englishman."

Suddenly, I felt quietly satisfied and somehow more confident.

School, Sorbonne & Jean-Claude

Next day I was busy preparing for the autumn term at my school. Being the youngest of the family, I believe in all honesty that I benefitted education-wise more than my brothers or sister. I suppose family fortunes had improved over the years and I think my parents wanted to give me the best education possible. Ironically, brother Alan won a scholarship to attend an excellent grammar school, Leyton County High and went on to Oxford, attaining top honours and, subsequently, following a career in Law. I studied but not with the same enthusiasm and dedication. I preferred playing tennis and cricket and tended to neglect the very subjects I should have worked harder at. However, when I was in junior school, Essex House, I had the dubious honour of giving a future Wimbledon finalist Christine Truman her very first tennis lesson, and later, at the City of London School, I was in the first eleven cricket team playing alongside the future England captain— Mike Brearley.

The school term started with most of the pupils looking smart in their new or nearly new uniforms, white shirts and school tie. My least favourite subjects were Mathematics, Physics and Chemistry, but I enjoyed languages and concentrated on French, German, English history and English language. I was looking forward to the French lesson because the teacher in charge, Mr Whitmore, was good at spotting pupils who were trying hard but who lacked that special talent. For some unknown reason, he pointed his finger at me and said, "Anderson, read the following paragraph!"

He threw a typewritten piece from Molière on to my desk. I went ahead, and after about thirty seconds, he stopped me and said, "Anderson, have you spent time in France during the holidays?"

I replied, "Yes, Sir."

He then went on to ask me if I had spent time in the southwest of France. How on earth could he have known that because I had told no one at school?

"How did you know, Sir?" I asked.

"Because of the way you pronounced '*Eh bien*' and other words. You have certainly made remarkable progress. Well done, Anderson."

I was delighted and enormously proud. I felt that my month in Brive was now paying off. The whole of that term, I worked particularly hard at my French and came top of the class. I was presented with my school prize by the Lord Mayor of London, Sir Denys Lowson at the annual prize-giving ceremony.

I passed five O levels and even though later I sat and failed my A levels; I felt that with a little more effort I could have succeeded and perhaps gone on to an English university. However, I was not too sure in which direction I should proceed, so when I spoke to our German teacher, Dr Law-Robertson, he said "Look, Graham, you have failed your A levels which may prevent you from going to university but you have a very smart appearance. You are very polite so I feel you need a position which will complement your affable and easygoing manner with people. May I suggest you speak to the careers representative who will be here at the end of term to discuss your next move?"

I was called into the office by the careers adviser and amongst various other suggestions, it was put to me that managerial training schemes at Marks and Spencer were available with a view to becoming a manager in one of their branches. Somehow this did not appeal to me, but it was something my German master said to me that persuaded me to move in another direction. He said that my French was excellent and my German passable and thought that a career in the hospitality industry, such as running a hotel would suit me. Still at school, I managed to satisfy the requirements of the Sorbonne University and I secured a place at this world-renowned institution to study *'l'Histoire de la Culture et la Civilisation Française'* but that would not commence until the spring term.

I left school at nearly eighteen years of age and had so much to look forward to. First of all, I had to make plans for my studies at the Sorbonne in Paris. From my contact in the Modern Languages department, I secured an address within walking distance of the Sorbonne, where an elderly lady had a spare room available. Thus, my future was taking shape and I was looking forward to this new challenge. France had always fascinated me even when my parents took my brother Alan and me on holiday to Juan-les-Pins in the South of France for the very first time. And now I was about to leave my family at a time when coffee bars suddenly sprang up everywhere in England, so this new innovation gave me the opportunity to meet other young people of the same age and discuss topics that were prevalent at the time, particularly when one is slipping out of immaturity into adulthood. One person I got to know well through the Calypso was a French student, another Jean-Claude. I found out that he had in fact been staying in lodgings in Chingford with an English family, all arranged again by Mrs Rooney, the French lady teacher. Being a year older than me, Jean-Claude had a great deal more experience of life than I did. He was in the habit of frequenting two nightclubs around Soho and Green Park— *La Côte D'Azur* and *Le Contemporain*. I had never before been to the West End on my own, let alone frequenting nightclubs, so to the concern of my parents and the approval of Jean-Claude, he encouraged me to see what I was missing out on. From Woodford to Oxford Circus, it involved taking a train from Snaresbrook on the Central Line to get to the places than Jean-Claude raved about. Also, he liked me being with him because his English was extremely limited, and I think he wanted to introduce me to a life that I had never experienced before. I was not used to drinking and being surrounded by so many attractive young people—women in particular who seemed to be attracted to Jean-Claude whom the French would describe as *'un beau parleur'* (a real smoothie, absolute charmer). He would never master English because apart from trying a few simple English words with me and my family, he would by choice only speak French. Socially he preferred mixing with his fellow compatriots. Another centre of French influence was a coffee bar in Dean St, Soho called *Les Enfants Terribles*. I cannot remember how many times I travelled with him to London but he, invariably would remain overnight in the West End and spend the entire night with a beautiful girl, and I, as usual, would travel home alone. On another occasion there was an embarrassing moment on a crowded train during rush hour. As so often happened between stations, the train would come to a complete standstill between Mile End station and Leytonstone. Unlike today where we have mobile phones and noisy music there was absolute silence in the packed train. It is a very British silence—no conversation and passengers hiding behind their *Evening Star* or *Standard* newspaper. It was during one of these stops that Jean-Claude caused, quite unintentionally, a bit of a rumpus. He simply said to me that he wanted to see a French film by the famous producer Pierre Billon that was showing in London. *"Je veux voir le film qui s'appelle 'Mon phoque et moi'"* (my seal and me). He was recommending a film to me containing the word *'phoque'* which obviously is pronounced exactly the same way as the English swearword. Now people were abandoning their newspapers and one man shouted, "No bad language! Can't you see there are ladies present?"

With great impatience Jean-Claude kept repeating this title three times thinking I did not understand, which only made matters worse. I whispered in his ear to tell him *'phoque'* sounds like an offensive English word. He understood. I smiled at the man who took offence and I said, "He's from Paris." A bit like Basil Fawlty describing Manuel in *Fawlty Towers* by adding, "he's from Barcelona".

Jean-Claude's reputation at *Les Enfants Terribles* was well-known amongst all the students and especially the women around Soho. In fairness to him he never resorted to paying for his sexual appetite, but I would bet that the women who normally do charge for such a service would have been only too willing to pay *him*. Such were his good looks and charm. The next day I received a frantic call from him. He urgently wanted to come around to see me and said he was going to ask me a big favour. I had no idea what was going on, so I told him to come to my parents' house and explain what had happened. He said that he was in the habit of writing home to his parents in Paris every week and at the same time sending a letter to a male friend. He had the unfortunate habit of writing both letters one after the other and then writing the envelopes separately. Unfortunately for him the letter destined for his friend finished up in the envelope addressed to his mother. In it he described how many women he was bedding every week, how his advancement in English was zero and in addition to this he had lost twelve kilos in weight. When his mother opened the misdirected letter, she was naturally fuming with rage. Therefore, she decided to get on the first Air France plane available and travel to see him with her elder son, Roger. They would be staying at the Strand Palace Hotel for two nights to see what their promiscuous family member was up to. I wondered what I could do to help him. He knew right away. He said he wanted me to put on my old City of London school blazer, plaster down my hair with Brylcreem with a side parting and in general take on the appearance of a serious companion and student. I got my mother to sew on to my old school blazer, a rather posh-looking badge with the words in Latin *'Dominus dirige nos'* (Oh, dear Lord guide us).

At the pre-arranged meeting, Jean-Claude and I turned up at the reception of the Strand Palace Hotel on time. We were met at reception by Jean-Claude's mother, Madame Lecoin and the elder brother Roger. I caught a glimpse of myself in the full-length mirror just before going into the dining room. I had never seen myself looking so ridiculous. There I was with nicely razor-edged pressed grey trousers, school blazer and tie, shiny black patent-leather shoes and hair plastered down with Brylcreem. As they were Parisians, that meant a total of four kisses—two on both cheeks. I noticed Madame Lecoin looking at Jean-Claude in a reprimanding way, but nothing was said until we adjourned to the dining room. To make conversation Roger said he was very impressed with my French, which made me feel more at ease. I told him that Jean-Claude had made enormous strides in English which pleased them both. I was, obviously, lying through my teeth. I had before this meeting taught Jean-Claude a few sentences in English parrot-fashion. This is how it went:

"Good morning. What is your name?"

"My name is Jean-Claude."

"What do you think of England?"

"I simply love the people and I want to come back next year."

Even though he did not know exactly what he was saying he was very convincing, and I know they were impressed. Nothing was said about the mix-up with the letters, but Madame Lecoin kept going on about how much weight he had lost and that it must be him missing French food. The rest of the evening went very well and all four of us went into the adjacent lounge for coffee. I think Madame and Roger were both impressed with my dreadful shiny plastered-back hair with a little side parting. I hated everything about my appearance, but the plan so far was working. They were only there for one more night, so mission was hopefully accomplished. I sat down in reception and allowed the three of them a little time to themselves. Madame pointed to a table some distance from me, and I noticed her face had taken on a more serious look. After half an hour all three reappeared, smiling, with Jean-Claude looking pleased with himself. Even after Madame and Roger left the next day, Jean-Claude never confided in me what was said at their family meeting. All he said was, *"Tu es un vrai copain, tu as bien fait"* —I was a true friend, and I did well.

After three weeks Jean-Claude returned to Paris to be with his family. I think he was grateful for my dressing up as a pathetic and immature Noël Coward to make my very impressionable appearance in front of his mother and brother, because he very kindly invited me to stay in Paris a few weeks later, which I did. Thinking that I would be accommodated wherever they lived, I was somewhat disappointed as the only accommodation they had was above their very busy delicatessen/boucherie shop, but that was filled to capacity with other members of the family. Therefore, Madame Lecoin at her own expense arranged for me to stay in a small *'Pension de famille'* in Montmartre. From their shop to my guest house took only minutes on the metro to a station called Jules Joffrin. Every day I took the train to Jean-Claude's family business and ate excellent food with them. For several weeks in August everything closes in Paris. The family closed their shop and disappeared to a rented home in Normandy in a town called Deauville. They took me with them. Jean-Claude's father had unfortunately been gassed during the last war which affected his breathing and – even worse – his driving. We all piled into the Renault Dauphine and it was Madame who had to instruct him when to turn left, turn right or go straight on. He was certainly the worst driver with whom I ever had the misfortune of being a passenger. He braked unnecessarily and was totally oblivious to traffic lights. This was well before the advent of seatbelts and on two occasions, I bashed my head against the back of the driver's seat when he braked suddenly for no apparent reason.

After several hours of trepidation on my part, the car eventually came to a standstill in front of a very imposing house with wrought-iron gates and a long driveway. I was so grateful to have arrived in one piece. We were greeted by a couple dressed very smartly. He, in a shiny dark suit and black tie and the lady in black as well with a crisp white pinafore. I suppose he could be described as a butler and his wife *'femme de ménage / cuisinière'*. This lady produced the most incredible food which opened my eyes again to the virtues of French cuisine. She would take me into her kitchen and show me so many different gastronomic dishes and how to prepare them. She was proud of her selection of so many cheeses and the various brands of cider and in particular, the apple brandy called Calvados. I personally only knew of Cheddar and Stilton cheese back home, but when I visited the nearby town of Honfleur and entered a *'fromagerie'* I quite honestly never thought there could be so many cheeses available in so many shapes, colours and sizes.

At lunch and dinner, Monsieur Lecoin would incessantly talk about his return to Paris and what fresh produce he planned to supply his shop with—new ideas about home-made *pâtés* which were so appreciated by their customers. I certainly was not looking forward to the car journey back to Paris. Anyway, that day came and went, and there I was back in Paris and about to depart the next day to England. All in one piece despite the frightful driving of Monsieur Lecoin. I did my usual courteous act and went to the next-door florist to buy Madame Lecoin a gorgeous bouquet of flowers, said my goodbyes to all the family and with my little suitcase made my way to the train station where I took the train to Calais. After the short boat journey to Dover, I then made three train changes and found my way to Snaresbrook Station where Dad was waiting for me. On the way home, Dad did not speak a great deal. In fact, he was not the sort of man to indulge in trivial conversation but if he had something to say then it would be said with conviction and frankness.

*   *   *   *

Dad pulled up in the drive of our house and Mum must have heard the car arriving, because she was there at the front door with a big smile and arms open to receive me. She hugged me furiously and said right away that I looked a different person to the one who left some time ago. I suppose it was now my second time away from the gentle but respectful show of parental discipline that I had got accustomed to. I felt I was now an adult. I can never forget the last advice my mother gave me before my trip to Paris. Mum had the ability of getting across her meaning without actually spelling it out. Before she kissed me goodbye she said, "Graham, you are a nice-looking young man, and you are going to Paris. You also have a rather dubious friend called Jean-Claude. I want you to return physically in the same way as you left!" Point taken, Mum!

Back in Essex there were a lot of foreign students, mostly French and Spanish who were staying in a place in Chigwell called Grange Farm. It provided basic accommodation but when young and inexperienced, single and unaccustomed to the luxuries of life, these foreign students were easy to please and found escapism in this environment, especially as there was a separate accommodation wing for housing female students from these two countries. This gave all foreign students the chance to meet and mingle with the local youth of Woodford. It was, at that time, also a chance of being able to meet people of my own age, both local and foreign. One evening I was in the Calypso coffee bar alone and could not help overhearing what a group of pretty young local girls were saying to each other. There was a lot of loud giggling and the theme of their conversation was how attractive they found the foreign male students compared to their English counterparts. One girl went even further in revealing in detail her experiences with at least three of the French students she had met recently in the coffee bar. She was with two other girls and was quite open and explicit about these experiences. They had their backs to me, but I could hear everything that was being said, and when the girl who was boasting about her sexual successes left the coffee bar, her two companions, carried on talking about her and criticising her frankness. One of them said, "I know we all drop our knickers from time to time but that is ridiculous."

I thought that such a statement was unnecessarily offensive especially when they had so unfairly compared their fellow English male contemporaries so unfavourably with the foreign students. I suddenly felt a little protective of my fellow countrymen, but I reluctantly agreed with some of the points of view of the young English girls' comments in the coffee bar. I became more observant of these foreign students and their behaviour and attitude towards the Anglo-Saxons. When they spoke it sounded like music to my ears. They were not static when they wished to make a point. They waved their hands about and I noticed that they would gently put a hand on the shoulder of a fellow male or gently tap the waist of a girl to stress what they were saying. There was nothing offensive about this behaviour, but it seemed alien to the observant English onlooker. I found these gestures full of charm, extravagance and knew it was not something I had been brought up to do.

One evening, a French student came into the Calypso and I saw two of his compatriots talking to two blonde local girls. This student—his name was Michel, went up to his French friends and exchanged four kisses on the cheek and his friends reciprocated. It was only the second time that I had seen such warmth between young men in a public place. To them it seemed perfectly normal, and I admired this openness and the fact that it came naturally to them: no fumbling about with wet little handshakes, blushing or self-consciousness but a bold Latin expression of warmth and sincerity. It was that very evening that I met and spoke to a young blonde lady who turned out to be a former fellow-pupil in the same class at St Mary's Convent in Woodford when we were both nine years of age. It was a meeting that would change my life, but more of that later.

The French and Spanish male students seemed less stiff and starchy than their English counterparts and even though they were casual with their way of dressing, they were not just smart but chic and attractive. I noticed how the local women looked up to them and amongst the youthful giggles that emanated from them when they could not understand the accent or meaning of a certain word, this only seemed to add to this mysterious and seductive charm. Michel and his friends wore tinted glasses, something I had only previously associated with Mafia bosses in Sicily or pensioners of a certain age who could not focus their eyes on a moving object. The next day I went out and bought my second pair of sunglasses. I told my parents that as I was going to study in France, I would need them. My mother must have thought that Paris was, weather-wise, a much hotter place than London.

*   *   *   *

Within a week I was on my way to Paris. I got off the train at Dover and boarded the cross-channel ferry that would take me to Calais. I had previously done the same journey with my parents and brother Alan many years previously, but this time I was eighteen years old and entirely on my own. While I was on the boat, I heard a young couple speaking to each other in an unusual language that I did not recognise. I could tell that they had only just met each other because of their body language. When I eventually spoke to the lady, she surprised me with an absolute clarity in English, but at the same time she had a slight but very attractive and charming accent. I then asked her what language she was speaking to the young man. I was shocked with her reply because she explained that she was speaking Welsh and he was speaking Breton, but they understood each other perfectly well, such is the close association between the two languages, both historically and culturally.

I got off the boat in Calais and made my way to the train station. Once on the train and having found my seat, I could smell the wonderful and pungent whiff of garlic and Gauloises again throughout the carriage. The man who was sharing a saucisson and tomato baguette with his wife was complimentary about my French. They wished me luck with my studies and scribbled their address on something resembling toilet paper. I had arrived several days too early to take up my accommodation with the elderly lady near the Sorbonne, so I went down to the Metro and bought a ticket for Place Pigalle where I knew there would be reasonably-priced accommodation. I had little money on me, so I had to spend three nights in a basic but clean *'pension de famille'*. On my last night there, I was not feeling too well and thought that I had a cold or chill coming on, so I went to bed to keep as warm as possible. The next day I was not much better, plus I now had a sore throat. After packing my little suitcase, I went downstairs to reception to pay for my accommodation. I saw the owner behind his desk, and I tried to ask him for the bill—*"je voudrais payer la facture, s'il vous plaît"* but absolutely nothing came out. I was, for the first time in my life, speechless. My voice had totally disappeared, and my throat was worse than ever. I paid the bill and with a gesture of waving my arms and making a thumbs-up sign, I left Place Pigalle and went straight to the Gare de Lyon. My mind was made up. There and then, I decided not to attend my course at the Sorbonne, so I would blame my absence on my lack of voice and a sore throat. It was a pitiful excuse and looking back I think, at the back of my mind there was the more enticing and seductive vision of spending time to recuperate in the South of France. Before I left England, my sister gave me an address in Roquebrune, where she had stayed a year before, so armed with this information, my next problem was to break the news to my parents and endeavour to convince them that I was doing the right thing.

I remember having to change trains, and I think it was the town of Montpellier where I then took another train to Monaco. Once again, there was the familiar smell of garlic and Gauloises. I now felt much more at ease, and I was convinced that I had made the right decision. I could feel the weather getting warmer, and suddenly everything seemed better. As the train slowed down, I recognised the actor Nigel Patrick walking along the platform with another actor whose claim to fame was a part in *The Cruel Sea*. I do not know his name. I can hear people asking, "Well, who the hell is Nigel Patrick?" You must be of a certain age to know the answer.

I grabbed my suitcase, left the train and made my way to the exit. I stopped an elderly lady and asked her where I could find the bus for the short journey to Roquebrune. She pointed to a bus stop that was just out of sight, and I made my way to it. Just five minutes later, the bus pulled up and I got on. The journey did not last long, about twenty minutes. The conductor kindly told me where to get off. On alighting from the bus, I found the surroundings quiet and peaceful. All I had in my hand was a piece of paper with the name of a certain Madame Béghelli written on it. In my other hand was my suitcase. It was more of a two-level crossroad where I got off the bus—the upper road, as I discovered later, would lead to Italy and the lower road to what was then a small village called Roquebrune. I then walked to the only shop I could see. In fact, it was a small estate agency tucked away on the lower road and, as the owner explained to me, Madame Béghelli lived on top of his shop up a very steep staircase which would take me to my home for the next five weeks. I knocked at the rickety old door and waited a good minute standing outside and wondering how I would be received, assuming there was a room available. As the door opened, there was a profound creaking noise as though it had not been opened in years. Over the next few weeks, I became quite accustomed to this painful noise. Suddenly there appeared a white-haired elderly lady with most of her teeth missing and a prominent lisp when she spoke. She wore a skirt with so many patches on it that there were more patches than the original cloth.

"Qu'est-ce que vous voulez?" she shouted at me.

I said that "my sister had stayed with you and had given me your address, so I was just wondering if you could accommodate me for the next six weeks". Of course, all this was said in French! The moment I mentioned the name 'Kitty', she stepped towards me and gave me a really fierce hug followed by a kiss on both cheeks. Fortunately, she was not born in Paris otherwise it would have meant two more supplementary kisses. She told me she had a room available and that it had a separate entrance of its own on the upper road that led to Italy, so she said I could then come and go as I pleased and would not disturb anybody with the creaking noise of that infernal downstairs door. She gave me the key to my room but not before she asked for a weeks' rent in advance. She went on to say that this arrangement would continue until my departure. She then led me to my room, which was not locked. She pushed open the door and showed me around. In those days, there were no en-suite facilities, so if I needed to go to the toilet, it meant leaving my room and walking down a narrow corridor, and the bathroom was there on the right, tucked away as if in a small alcove. I looked inside and despite its strange position, I could see that it was clean, as was my bedroom. With the accommodation came a breakfast of croissants and black coffee and in the evening a meal that I would have to eat alongside Mrs Béghelli's family. In fact, the only family members consisted of a son, Gaston, and her brother Louis. Gaston was crippled and had a dreadful physical handicap caused by a German military vehicle that ran over him on practically the last day of the war in 1945. He had just crossed the road to speak to a neighbour when it happened. As I would later discover, he was one bitter and resentful person. Mrs Béghelli's brother, Louis, was handicapped from birth, and extremely challenged psychologically and spent most of his time either nodding his head in agreement with Gaston or shaking it from left to right in anger. For a reason unknown to me, this sadly disabled man would shout, "*Oui, les emmerdeurs, les Anglais!*" (the shitty English). I felt that this was possibly due to an intensive indoctrination and bad influence he received from Gaston, who naturally was self-conscious about his physical condition. I sympathetically tried to understand the reason for his quick temper and resentment. However, he did not show any kindness towards me but continually went on about British Colonialism and the appalling treatment handed out to the Irish people by the British Government.

However, even though I argued with him and defended loyally whatever the English did, I listened intently to his harangues but in a strange way appreciated his logic, simply because I had never heard the other side of the story in the English–Irish historical confrontations and connotations. I was young, eighteen years of age and felt obliged to defend my English heritage come what may, even though I knew that our colonial history did have many dark corners and a history of invasion and domination.

I unpacked my suitcase in my bedroom and contemplated what my daily routine would be for the next six weeks. I had with me an old-fashioned little radio that my brother, Alan, had given me. I turned it on and suddenly felt emotional when I heard the song being played on my crackly little contraption—it was 'Freight Train', sung by Chas McDevitt and Nancy Whiskey. It made me really feel at home.

I soon found out how to get to Monte Carlo. There was a bus stop just a short distance from my lodgings and a bus service that stopped there every hour, so every day after breakfast, I would wait at the bus stop and then travel to Monte Carlo to buy an English newspaper that was always a day or two out of date. I would then sit down on a bench in front of the very luxurious Hotel de Paris. There I would read my newspaper in the sunshine as if I were a resident of this very pricey hotel. I would then walk a few yards down the road and find a small, inexpensive café where I would just sit watching all the people go by as I drank my coffee and finished reading my newspaper. I never really missed home in Woodford because I was truly happy with my new and different surroundings, and despite my love and feelings for my parents, I just could not believe my luck in being in such a beautiful and sophisticated place.

Madame Béghelli's family was bizarre and eccentric, but I grew to find them tolerable even though Gaston seemed to enjoy hurting people and criticising anything that was English. I think some of his political criticisms were justified but coming from a very conservative background as I did, I felt it was my obligation to defend the principles of the government of the day, however shaky they may have been. For sure, Gaston's observations and criticisms of the English government's attitude to the Irish question and its potential independence from Westminster have stayed with me to this day.

Part of Madame Béghelli's property at basement level was let to an estate agent, an Italian who was married to a lady from Wales, and they had a son named David. He was *'majordome'* to Sir Winston Churchill, a term that can be translated as butler. He was a nice, polite young man who enjoyed my company, I think because even though he spoke perfect English, as did his mother, he found talking to me a big change from having to speak French or Italian, languages in which he totally excelled. Sir Winston had a small house in Roquebrune, where during his retirement from politics, he spent most of his winters painting on canvas some of the beautiful scenery associated with the Alpes-Maritimes region. But more of this later.

On one of my trips to Monte Carlo, I decided to have *'une noisette'*—a small white coffee in one of the cafés near the *Hôtel de Paris*. At the next table was an elderly gentleman with a mass of white hair. He was tall and with age, stooping quite considerably. He was accompanied by a much younger lady with dark, short hair. I did not know the relationship between them as I was young and immature. They could have been married, or she could have been his daughter or maybe a private nurse, I thought. He was Italian, she was French. They both spoke good English, but he pronounced every word with a beautiful melodic accent. She spoke in a slightly harsher and more abrasive tone, which was reminiscent of a person from Marseille. In fact, when I got to know them better, she informed me that Marseille was the place of her birth. They both said how much they enjoyed my company and told me they would like to meet me again. I think they were impressed with my coming all this way from England just to learn French—or perhaps they were sympathetic to the fact that I was alone and staying in a basic room in a guest house with a well-known eccentric family. I learned that he was a retired film director called Vittorio, and her name was Simone. I am sure that Madame Béghelli's reputation must have reached the attention of my new-found friends, as they told me that they lived in a flat near the guest house of my weird family.

We became good friends. They invited me to their beautiful flat on several occasions, and I remember having tea and biscuits in their large, airy lounge, which overlooked the small village of Roquebrune—small at the time but now, all these years later, it is now bigger and more commercial. At the time, I did not think much about their invitations, but looking back and taking into consideration my present knowledge of customs abroad, I can honestly say that it was the first and only time anyone offered me tea and biscuits, such was their way of endeavouring to please me— they must have associated tea with England, because ever since then if I were offered hospitality in France, it would always be coffee— or perhaps a Pastis!

A Dubious Trip to Italy

On returning to my room, I saw Madame Béghelli standing outside my room talking to another tenant whose door was half-open. She said, "Gramm" (because she could not pronounce my name properly), "you said you wanted to buy some shoes in Italy, well this gentleman is Italian, and he goes regularly across the border and knows where all the best shops are."

I accepted his offer and thanked him. He said he would be going the next day, which pleased me, and he told me to be ready by ten o'clock.

I turned up the next day on time. I asked him his name, and he told me to call him Carlo. The journey to the Italian border from Roquebrune in his little Fiat 600 was brief without any hold-ups. We passed through the last French town of Menton in next to no time and then drove on to the border. Carlo could not speak a word of English, so naturally, we spoke French together. His French was shaky, with a heavy but musical turn of phrase. This gave me more confidence, and as an eighteen-year-old, I modestly considered my French to be better than his. However, I was really grateful for this lift because the bus service would have taken longer, and it would have cost me quite a few francs. I must say that his driving was full of confidence, and he drove extremely fast. He gave me the impression that he was permanently in a hurry and somewhat agitated. What follows now should be a warning to other young people. I was eighteen and utterly inexperienced and immature in every sense of the word. I was naturally grateful to be driven to Italy, but then Carlo made a strange request. He said that at the border, he was often stopped and questioned by the border guards, which he resented. He said he did not want me to get involved should he be stopped again. He told me he would stop his car some distance before the border, and once clear and having arrived on the other side, he would then proceed to pick me up after I had crossed on foot. He stopped the car as he said he would, but just before I got out, he said, "Put this in your pocket and give it back to me when I pick you up on the other side."

Put it down to naïveté or some other youthful weakness but I never thought it anything but polite to do as I was requested. I got out of the car just before the frontier, and he passed me a soft package which he told me to put in my pocket. I walked for about five minutes to get to the guarded frontier and had my passport checked by the uniformed official. He then stamped it, passed it back to me and then I continued my little walk into Italy to wait for Carlo to pick me up. I must have been walking for some eight minutes when I sensed a car slowing down parallel to me and the driver telling me to get inside. *"Bouge ton cul"* was his somewhat vulgar phrase, so I obeyed his command reluctantly. He then asked me to take the soft packet out of my pocket and hand it over to him, which I did. He then placed it under the driver's seat, and we immediately continued our journey into the busy border town of Ventimiglia. After about half an hour at the wheel, Carlo stopped the car in front of a café-cum-tobacconist. He leant down to pick up the mysterious packet from under his seat and proceeded to enter the café. At this point in my naïveté, I had the feeling that I was being used by this man, and I wanted to know what was going on. A minute later, he returned to the car, got in and at that very moment, I noticed a wad of lira notes in his tightly clasped hand. He put these under his seat with the packet – now considerably reduced in size – that I had brought across the border. He said nothing. I asked him what he was selling.

"Tu fermes ta gueule et tu dis rien à personne!" Ce n'est pas tes oignons" —basically, he told me to shut my gob, say nothing to anybody, and to mind my own business.

He shouted, "You wanted to buy some cheap Italian shoes, and that is why you cadged a lift!"

We then continued on to our next stop, which was San Remo. Once again, he took with him the soft packet from under his seat and entered a scruffy-looking café. Next to the café was a shoe shop, so I got out of the car and went inside, tried on a pair of suede shoes, paid for them and went back to the car. The atmosphere was tense. I did not want to speak to Carlo anymore because I knew that he had used me for his nefarious deeds. He got into the car, plonked himself into the driver's seat and put an ever more diminished packet under his seat. I assumed that he had one more delivery to make with whatever was left in the packet. Ten minutes later, he stopped at a third café and very quickly did what he had to do and returned hastily to the car, his fist clenched around lira notes, which this time he put into his pocket. He then turned the car around, and we made off to the French border. We showed our respective passports to the border control and proceeded to drive back, passing again through Menton and finally arriving in Roquebrune. There was absolute silence all the way home, except for one occasion, when, sensing that I was not happy with his behaviour, he endeavoured to make trivial conversation, which I totally ignored. We arrived back at the guest house, and it was only then that I realised how very naïve I had been and, above all, stupid. Stupid to have been inadvertently a carrier of illegal drugs and brave enough to warn Carlo that one day he would finish up in one of Italy's notorious jails. I got out of the car and from that moment onwards every time I saw him, I completely ignored him. Some days later, Madame Béghelli did in fact tell me that he was a man not to be trusted and that I should be wary of him. Better late than never! After this episode, I had nothing more to do with him. Looking back on this experience, it should be a warning to any young, impressionable and naïve person who could innocently finish up in jail through no fault of his own. This was an experience I'll never forget and one which other youngsters should learn from.

A Brief Encounter

The next day Madame Béghelli knocked at my bedroom door and said that there was a lady asking for me downstairs. I followed her into her scruffy parlour, and I immediately recognised the pretty lady standing in the doorway. It was Simone, the companion of the Italian film director, Vittorio, who made me so welcome when I paid them a visit and had tea and biscuits with them. I was shocked that such a smart lady would ever be seen in such a hovel.

"Qu'est-ce que vous faites là?" I asked her, longing to know what she wanted and what she was doing in this Godforsaken place. I saw her wink at Madame Béghelli when she told me to use the familiar *'tu'* form instead of *'vous'*. I still did not understand the relationship between Simone, who I think was in her early forties and the film director, Vittorio. Could she be his nurse? Or did they have some stronger and closer relationship that I was unaware of? I asked her about Vittorio and enquired about his health.

"Il est fatigué il ne veut pas sortir et il pique en ce moment un petit roupillon," she said, explaining that he was tired, did not want to go out and was having a nap. She went on to say that she was free that afternoon, so suggested that we should both go to the beach and sunbathe. I said that I was doing nothing in particular and agreed that we should do just that. We walked to the nearest bus stop, waited a few minutes and then jumped on the bus that took us quickly to the beach. The day was extremely hot, and strangely enough, the beach was not too crowded. As we walked along a sandy stretch of beach, I somehow felt her getting closer to me, slightly leaning against me and then taking my hand in hers and putting her fingers in a clenched and intertwining clasp with my own fingers. I suddenly felt uncomfortable and pulled my hand away, only for her to grab it again, and this went on for several minutes until I made a decision to say that it was time for me to return home.

"*D'accord,*" she replied as she pulled me towards her and kissed me softly on both cheeks. I had just turned eighteen and was inexperienced about life, but at the same time, I had such affection for Vittorio that I did not want my respect for him to be tarnished by some indiscretion on my part. I went up to my room, and I remembered that I had bought a small half-bottle of Côtes du Rhône wine the last time I went into Monaco. All I had was an empty coffee cup, no glass, so I drank from the cup, and suddenly I felt more relaxed thinking again about my afternoon and of how much I had grown up. Perhaps it was the wine, but I felt sleepy. I was thinking about dinner because I was hungry. Madame Béghelli had suggested that for a few more francs I could eat with her family every evening. She knew that her son annoyed me, and her brother insulted me frequently, but I think she had a good heart. Even though the surroundings, especially the kitchen, were scruffy, I enjoyed the food that she cooked. The first thing I noticed was that beef and lamb were never overcooked and there was always an abundance of pasta adorned with tomatoes and garlic. I suppose being so close to Italy, there was an interchange of recipes covering both countries. There was an enormous number of salads, tomatoes, onions, garlic, courgettes, gherkins and red peppers all smothered generously with virgin olive oil.

Trip to Monte Carlo

The estate agent's son, David, popped in to speak to Madame Béghelli about a problem with drips of water emanating from her property and penetrating the ceiling in his father's office below. While he was investigating the origins of this seepage, I came down and to my surprise, Gaston offered me a Pastis, a drink I had never tried before. I said I would like to have a glass which he filled with loads of ice, Pastis and then topped up with good cold water and then I saw the drink change colour. The taste was agreeable, but I noticed he did not offer David a drink.

David said he had a free morning the next day and asked me if I would like to go on the bus with him to Monaco. I agreed and he asked me to be ready by ten o'clock. As promised, the next day, David arrived on time, and I was ready and waiting for him downstairs just outside his father's agency. We jumped on the bus which left at 11.15 a.m. The twenty-minute journey passed very quickly because David was talking about his love for this region of France and stated how happy he was with his employment in Roquebrune. We jumped off the bus together and went to buy the English newspapers, which in those days were delivered a day late but it was a good way of keeping up with the news. I noticed that David bought the *Times* newspaper which made me think that perhaps he was more serious than I had at first thought. I bought the *Daily Express*, so I wondered if I would go down in his estimation of me. However, he pointed to a nearby café and so we then sat down outside in the very pleasant early morning sunshine and waited to be served. At that point, my mind went back to Woodford and the two pubs there, the Horse and Well and The Travellers' Friend, where if you wanted a drink or a bag of crisps or peanuts, you had to queue up, wait your turn and instantly pay before you even sip your first gulp. So, this idea of getting served and sitting at a table as long as you were spending money was completely new to me and I appreciated the confidence the café had in its clientele, not fearing that we were about to run away after consuming our coffee. I then was inquisitive as to how David came to live and work in this beautiful region of France and what he did for a living. He said that his mother was Welsh and that his Dad was Italian but did not say where his parents had actually met. The coffees came. He had a black coffee, I had a *'noisette'*.

"David, may I ask you what you do for a living?" I asked.

"I work for Sir Winston Churchill," he replied.

This took me aback somewhat. Not because he was incapable of doing whatever he did for Sir Winston, but I thought on meeting him for the very first time that he would not look out of place working in a luxury hotel like the nearby Hotel de Paris or in an upmarket Michelin-starred restaurant. He was impeccably dressed even when he was not working, and his manners had that touch of class that one was not accustomed to seeing in a person of his age. I guessed he was in his early twenties. I was frankly surprised but delighted that he was actually working for such a high-profile person.

Even though my French had improved enormously, it was just enjoyable to express myself in my own language with someone who, I think, felt the same, even though David was totally fluent in both French and Italian and, needless to say, English. I thought I would ask him about his job and how he came to be living in Roquebrune. I suspected from our conversation that his father, being Italian, may have been a prisoner of war in Wales, so that could be how his mother met her future husband. Perhaps that could be due to my suspicious and inquisitive mind, and I may be totally wrong on this matter, but because he did not reveal precisely how or when or where his parents met; I just felt that there was a reluctance on his part to tell me the whole story. It just did not add up. For me, it did not matter because he was a decent man with impeccable manners and was employed by arguably one of the greatest statesmen ever. I wanted to know what routine his work involved in the service of Sir

Winston. He told me that he had worked for Sir Winston for two years and that his job involved some interesting aspects that surprised me. Sir Winston was not just a politician known universally but someone who loved working with water colours and was a painter of considerable talent, with some of his portraits universally recognised in the world of art. David said that at night he would accompany Sir Winston to his bedside, place him gently on the bed and then would put two small handkerchiefs, which had previously been soaked in hot water and wrung out, and place them over his eyes. Sir Winston said the warmth of the material over his eyes made him envisage the palm trees and other beautiful scenes that he would be painting the next day. David said that Sir Winston insisted that this unusual process helped to inspire his artistic creativity.

I told David that I too had something in common with his employer and that my only claim to fame with the great man was the fact that I came from Woodford Green, had lived there all my life and that our local parliamentary Member of Parliament had in the past been none other than Sir Winston himself. On hearing this news, David looked surprised and said nothing more. We finished our coffee and made our way home on the bus.

French Subjunctives

Back in my little room, I looked up in my Collins dictionary every word I used in my conversation with David and immediately translated every word into French along with their obligatory verbs. I learnt them all by heart, but at that time, as most aspiring linguists will remember, there was the hovering, menacing and ever-present novices' nightmare—the subjunctive, the mood of doubt. At that time, it still presented me with a headache. The English language has very few examples of the subjunctive, for instance, "if I were you" instead of the usual "if I was you", which really offends my ear. The French language has a plethora of subjunctives. I have observed that the French also try to avoid using it and find all manner of tricks to circumvent it. The reason for the English having fewer subjunctives is because, according to one cynic, the English are more sure of themselves. My mind goes back to my French master at school, Mr Whitmore, who said to me one day, "Anderson, *je viens à l'école chaque matin*; now you know I come to school every morning to teach the likes of you lot! Now give me a negative subjunctive to tell me that you doubted my coming every day."

I started fumbling my words… *"Je ne pense pas que vous…"* and then I was lost.

He bellowed at me, *"Je doute que vous puissiez venir ici tous les jours".* That is one phrase that, to this day, I have never forgotten. Then there is the imperfect subjunctive which is rarely used in everyday French. For those advanced students, here is a beauty, but be careful because it has a double meaning that makes a cynical French person cringe or laugh. Here goes: "If I had to know" becomes *"eût-il fallu que je le susse".* *'Suce'* is the subjunctive of *'savoir'* (to know) but also means something else that may be derogatory and taken the wrong way—so be careful.

That evening I went downstairs to eat with the family, and again the conversation turned political and once more, the topic of Ireland cropped up again. However, I was not in the mood for political discussion, so I kept my silence, had my pasta and beef dinner, thanked Madame Béghelli, then went upstairs to write a letter home to my parents.

My Refusal to Meet Sir Winston Churchill

The following day around nine o'clock I was awakened by Madame Béghelli, knocking at my door shouting that David was downstairs and that he wanted to talk to me. It sounded quite urgent, so I skipped taking my shower and made my way downstairs. Madame Béghelli was busy with a pair of nail clippers trimming the beautiful bougainvillaea that had wrapped itself around a rusty and crumbling piece of guttering. As I passed by her, she just said *"Bonjour"*, nothing more. There was at times a certain distance between us but at the same time she was kind to me, fed me well, and even though the food was simple and substantial peasant food, I appreciated everything she put before me.

I saw David standing in the kitchen. He said to me, "Graham I have a surprise for you. Yesterday you told me that you lived in the same constituency where Sir Winston was your Member of Parliament."

"Yes, David that is true. I remember telling you that yesterday," I replied.

"Well, I just happened to tell Sir Winston that I met a young student from Woodford and that we had a coffee together in Monaco."

"From Woodford? I know it well-that was my constituency when I was a Member of Parliament. I would like to meet this young man and introduce him to Lady Churchill and show him my paintings," Sir Winston had reportedly replied.

I was speechless, which was unusual for me. I could not speak and when I did, I do not think that David was very impressed with my reaction. At the back of my mind, I remember trying unsuccessfully, some years before, pinning a 'Vote Conservative' banner with a two-inch nail on to one of Dad's Sweet William pear trees in the front garden, just before the election on 26 May 1955. As it happened, there was a stiff breeze that kept tearing away and displacing the banner, which fell to the floor, then it started to rain, so I gave up. My father was Conservative both in politics and also in his demeanour, which along with his reserve, kindness and modesty towards people, made him shine amongst his contemporaries.

"That is so kind of him, David; I really appreciate this invitation," I said.

"Is that all you can say?" replied David, "it's not every day that you get invited to afternoon tea with such a distinguished world statesman!"

"What more do you want me to say?" I replied, feeling a little disgruntled by his comment.

"Lady Churchill said she will put on a special afternoon English tea with sandwiches and cakes for you and Sir Winston," David replied, saying that he too would be there, ready with a camera to record this special event and to supervise and serve the typical English tea but accompanied by French pâtisserie. David was a little surprised by my reaction and perhaps my reticence in offering him my immediate acceptance of this very special invitation. I went to my room and considered my position. I was almost eighteen years of age, and apart from being brought up in a very Conservative family, I really did not have that adequate and necessary experience for political discussion that would warrant a meeting with the great man himself. In fact, I was quite inexperienced in every facet of life. Perhaps, at that time, I felt inadequate, self-conscious and lacking the confidence to take part in this meeting. The very last thing I wanted was that Sir Winston should feel snubbed or humiliated, so I had to come up with an idea that would avoid this meeting taking place. I went to bed that night with a heavy heart, but I had made up my mind. The next morning Madame Béghelli knocked at my door and told me that David was waiting for me downstairs. I showered, got dressed and went downstairs. Again, Madame Béghelli was fiddling with that damn bougainvillea.

"Graham, everything is organised for tomorrow. I've ordered the cakes from the *pâtisserie* that Lady Churchill always has, and you are expected around three o'clock. No later because Sir Winston often has a nap in the afternoon. I'll come and get you as you do not know where we live. I also have a film ready for my camera because that is what Sir Winston would like."

I felt totally deflated, sad, and I could tell by the look on David's face that he expected bad news.

"David, I'm sorry, but I cannot come," I replied.

"You *what?*" he replied in utter disbelief. "You are turning down a meeting with perhaps the most famous person in the world; are you mad?"

"My father has been taken ill with a heart condition, so I have to go home and be with him," I replied.

He seemed more sympathetic on hearing this sad news and more so when I said I had to get a ticket to fly home from Nice Airport.

As a butler, I would guess that his position covers many sensitive situations, so I sympathised with him in that it was not in his remit to break the news to his employer that this almost eighteen-year-old would not be coming to the tea party. Some days later, when David was visiting his father's agency, he saw me coming down the stairs.

"I thought you were on your way home to be with your sick father?" he shouted.

I replied, "David, I have to be honest with you. My father is in good health, and I lied to you."

The look on his face was one of disbelief.

"Why, why, why?" he repeated angrily.

I replied, "David, please calm down. I know this is going to be the biggest mistake of my life, but I just could not go through with it. Why? Because I am incapable and inexperienced in dealing with a person of his calibre, his political acumen and fame. My mind went back to the day the world witnessed the presence of Sir Winston on the balcony of Buckingham Palace in 1945, along with the King and Queen, waving to the thousands of cheering people."

I continued, "Basically, I feel inadequate, immature and too shy and reserved to be in the company of a man who was so forthright and persuasive with words. And I feel and fear that I would be unable to arouse an interest conversation-wise in such distinguished company, with my pathetic knowledge of politics and my inability to talk at the same level as Sir Winston and Lady Churchill."

For a moment, he looked at me more sympathetically, which put my mind at rest. Compared to the suppressed anger he showed when I first informed him of my refusal to meet Sir Winston, he seemed more understanding of my predicament and sympathetic to my being so honest. Above all, I did not want to offend him or get him into trouble with his very famous employer. After this minor confrontation, we did meet occasionally but more by chance outside his father's agency. I understood his anguish. Here I was, a young man basically refusing a social meeting with possibly the most admired and distinguished world leader. In fact, it was Sir Winston who personally and along with his wife Clementine actually invited me, this young man from Essex, just because he heard it from David's lips. If this got David into trouble with his employer, I did, at the time, express my regret as best as I could. Understandably, our relationship was never quite the same after these unfortunate events. I never did ask him if there had been any reaction from Sir Winston, and he never spoke about this matter again. I just wanted to put the entire episode behind me and get on with the purpose of my visit—and that was to speak French fluently.

Farewell to my Eccentric French Family

I stayed in Roquebrune for five weeks. It was really my first time as an adult in a foreign country, and it turned out to be a turning point in my so-far sheltered life. I gained more confidence and felt more grown-up and mature. This was evident when on one occasion, I went into Monaco and got chatting to some British holidaymakers. At that time, the Brits were not too eager to speak a foreign language, so when I was asked to join two married couples from Surrey at their table, I put on my best French and ordered on their behalf four *'noisettes'* and a black coffee for me. They were very impressed with my performance and went on to ask me to translate and write down sentences they needed for the hotel where they were staying, such as the need for extra pillows, and directions to the bank, and other requirements. They asked me how much they should leave the waitress as a tip. I said that I would take care of that. *"C'est moi qui m'en occupe."*

Back home at my *'pension de famille'*, I spoke to Gaston about getting a job in or near Monaco. He avoided the subject and managed to divert my request and went on waffling about British Colonial policy and in particular, the situation in Ireland. I could not take any more. He realised that I was angry, and he tried to soften his approach. Eventually, he came around to answering my question by telling me that a local plastics factory nearby always needed employees. I wrote down the name of the company and went to my room. I found that a really excellent way of improving my French was to read the daily local newspaper. There was always one downstairs on the table next to a very old and decrepit stove. Madame Béghelli would always allow me to take the paper with me, on condition that it had to be returned before Gaston sat down to his lunch or his supper. He had the habitual routine of scrutinising every page meticulously, and whenever he came across an article that displeased him, he would grunt and utter his usual expletive *'putain de merde'*.

RESIDENTIAL RESTAURANT LICENCE   HOTEL REGISTER ⊗⊗

The Mornington
Hotel Limited

DON ROAD • ST. HELIER • JERSEY • JE2 4QD • CHANNEL ISLANDS

Proprietor & Managing Director: Mr. G. H. Anderson, A.I.L.
Telephone: 01534 - 24452   Facsimile: 01534 - 34131

27th Feb 2001.

Mr Winston Churchill M.P.
House of Commons,
Westminster.

Dear Sir,
    The reason I am writing to you is that I would not like to go down in history as the man who snubbed your great grandfather Sir Winston Churchill. As a young student of French, I very foolishly abandoned a place at the Sorbonne to seek the Sunshine and pleasures of "la Côte d'Azur." I stayed in a "pension de famille" which was cheap and cheerful but affordable. This would be around 1955. However to cut a long story short I stayed in Roquebrune for some six weeks and met a young man named David (whose mother was Welch, father Italian) and we became friends. When he told me that he was a butler/valet to your grandfather, w had a villa in Roquebrune I casually mentioned David that in fact I came from Woodford and that Sir Winston was in fact our local member of Parliament and that I saw him on one occasion giving a speech on the green in Woodford.

50

RESIDENTIAL RESTAURANT LICENCE   HOTEL REGISTER ☺☺

The Mornington Hotel Limited

DON ROAD   •   ST. HELIER   •   JERSEY   •   JE2 4QD   •   CHANNEL ISLANDS
Proprietor & Managing Director: Mr. G. H. Anderson, A.I.L.
Telephone: 01534 - 24452   Facsimile: 01534 - 34131

I was fascinated by the wonderful anecdotes that David would recall – for instance to help your grandfather create in his mind paintings that he would tackle the following day, my friend used to soak two small flannels in very hot water, wring them out and then place them over Sir Winston's eyes. Your grandfather said it inspired him to choose the following day's subject.

When David told your grandfather that there was a young student in the village (believe me Roquebrune at that time was more like a hamlet) who came from Woodford, Sir Winston immediately and very kindly arranged for David to bring me along to have tea with him. I think I was so overwhelmed and perhaps politically immature that I made an excuse not to go, and have regretted this blunder ever since – "les prasones de la jeunesse!"

I am sure that I deserve to be snubbed also after my appalling "faux pas" by your good self. Anyway I have overcome my youthful shyness. Hence my letter to you.

Yours Sincerely
Graham Anderson

51

37 ST. JAMES'S STREET
LONDON SW1A 1JG

19 April 2001

Dear Mr. Anderson,

Very many thanks for your recent letter, which was forwarded to me by the *Sunday Telegraph*.

I was most interested to hear your recollections of France during the 1950s, when you so nearly met my Grandfather!

With best wishes,

Yours sincerely,

Winston S. Churchill

G.H. Anderson, Esq.,
Proprietor & Managing Director,
The Mornington Hotel Limited,
Don Road,
St. Helier,
Jersey, JE2 4QD
Channel Islands.

The next day I went to the nearby plastics factory and made my way to the office. I asked a somewhat matronly lady if there were any jobs available.

"*Oui, toujours!*" she replied.

So that was encouraging. She sent me through to a larger room from where I could see a lot of activity beyond a dirt-stained window. There was a certain smell that was unpleasant, but I thought that if I got a job there, then I would have to get used to it. There was a short, fat man with receding hair fingering a packet of Gitanes cigarettes. He already had half of one plastered to the side of his red, bulbous lips. He shouted at me from his desk, "*Qu'est-ce que vous voulez?*"

I said I was looking for a job.

He must have heard that my accent was different. He said gruffly, "You are not French."

I said, "No, I am English."

"Well then," he went on, "we only employ French people in this factory." He pointed towards the door from where I had entered. I got the message, so I left and returned to my room a little dejected. My hopes of staying in such a beautiful region of France were dashed.

Altogether I stayed in Roquebrune for five weeks. My French certainly had improved because, apart from speaking English to Sir Winston's butler, David, I had no other contact with the English language, except for the odd encounter with fellow Brits in one of Monaco's cafés. As my time was coming to an end, I carried out the little act of courtesy that my mother had instilled in me from my first visit to Brive—that was to visit the florist, buy a thank-you card and present a beautiful bouquet to Madame Béghelli. She was quite touched when I gave her the very attractive assortment of flowers tied with a pink ribbon. I traced a tear in her eye as she pulled me towards her and kissed me on both cheeks. Gaston and Antoine just looked on grudgingly. I never ever saw her kiss either of them, so they were perhaps jealous that this young upstart from England was monopolising and getting in the way of their humdrum domestic routine. As I left to go to my room, I heard Gaston whisper, "*Espèce de tantouse"*, French for "what a poof". Just because I had given his mother flowers!

On the day of departure, I said my farewells to the three of them. More kisses from Madame Béghelli and just a reluctant handshake from Gaston. Nothing from Antoine except the usual cursory phrase, *"Putain de merde. Ces anglais m'emmerdent"*. I appreciate that he was mentally disabled and had been like that since birth, but all he did was copy the foul words and disagreeable behaviour of Gaston and repeat his obscenities.

However, I put my hand on his shoulder, wished him luck and said, *"à la prochaine"*.

I dragged my case down the stairway and went to the bus stop just across the road. As I stood waiting for the bus to Monaco, a neighbour, to whom I regularly said *'bonjour'*, waved to me from her car but did not stop. I knew this was her regular trip to the supermarket in Monaco and just wondered why she did not stop to give me a lift. For a moment, I suddenly thought how good it would be to see my family again in Woodford.

Return to Blighty

The journey home was uneventful. I arrived at Euston Station and saw my father waiting for me in his new MG Magnette. I suddenly felt very close to him. The car pulled into the driveway of our house, and everyone was there except brother Alan, who I think was away doing his national service. After the usual and anticipated conversation about my stay in *Le Midi*, life seemed to return to normal, but somehow, I already missed Roquebrune desperately. I suppose as an adult, it was the first time I had really been so alone and having to fend for myself, but also to experience that newly acquired personal freedom. Now that I was back in my room under the same roof as my family, I did feel somewhat restricted. It was not a case of my parents being intrusive in my lifestyle, but it was a reminder that I enjoyed my own company, which also allowed me, if I so desired, to pick and choose people whom I wanted to be with.

Before going to Roquebrune, I did pop into what was the latest fashionable craze at that time—the espresso coffee bar in Woodford, the Calypso. This had opened just before I left for France, and on entering, it seemed that time had stood still. It was packed with what seemed the same faces I saw before leaving the last time. There was a sprinkling of new French boys and girls staying at Grange Farm, here to improve their English. I noticed right away that these students were dressed again in such a stylish way that I instantly knew that they were not English. They reminded me of the people I used to see and speak to in Monaco, people with a certain charm and ebullience that I felt was lacking in my own compatriots. My mind went back to my time in Paris when Jean-Claude's brother, Roger, said that they could always recognise English women by their clothes. I took this at first as a compliment and replied, "Yes, they are well-dressed."

He pulled a face and said, "When I say I can recognise them by their clothes, it is because they are so badly dressed."

For a moment, that comment really hurt me, but I realised that he could be right. It was simply my defensive and automatic blind support for my own fellow Brits that made me think otherwise later on in my life. On another occasion, Jean-Claude's brother Roger said to me that, *"la télévision française est plus nette que celle d' Angleterre"* —"No, English television is just as clear screen-wise as French television-perhaps even more detailed and clearer."

I was so defensive of my country, but in the end, I had to admit that he was right as technically speaking, there were more numerous and finer screen lines on French television that did, in fact, produce a better picture. I had a similar run-in with Gaston in Roquebrune.

I knew just a little about Cromwell, the Irish question or how badly the Catholics were treated by the English but defend our history, I did with a vengeance. I was politically naïve, which made me think that history, whichever country writes about it, is tuned in to the general belief that an invented, a more favourable anecdote is preferable to the historical truth. Leaving England had really given me a short, sharp lesson in finding out more about myself and my country, which I do not think would have been evident had I spent all my youthful life in England.

In the Calypso coffee bar, I heard French being spoken, so I deliberately approached a group of students and came out confidently with my best French in introducing myself. *"Putain, enfin un vrai rosbif qui sait bien se démerder en français."*

They were surprised by my fluency and paid me a compliment in very slangy French, so during the next hour, I learnt that some of them came from Paris, the others from Auvergne and Périgord. I finished my coffee, said goodbye to the French students, and then I noticed that by now the café had become less crowded and I could actually see the people who were now seated on the benches next to the wall. By chance, I recognised the tall blonde lady who had been in my class at St Mary's Convent and to whom I had spoken just before I left for France. It was a meeting that would change my life. Her name was Sandra, and I arranged to meet her the following day. I knew that she lived in Woodford, somewhere near a railway station, so to make it easier for me, I suggested we meet at the same place, sometime the next day at the Calypso. From the following evening onwards, we saw each other about three times a week. She was working at a record shop in London called Imhofs, and I, in the meantime, took on a temporary position with the travel agent Thomas Cook. Previously to this, I worked as a trainee pastry cook at Lyons Corner House. Through my careers master at school, I had also been offered a place at Battersea College of Hotel Management to study every aspect of catering and management, with a view to eventually running a hotel belonging to one of the big hotel groups sometime in the future. It was a big mistake on my part because I desperately wanted to work in the kitchen of a quality restaurant and learn the basics of French cooking and how to produce some of the wonderful recipes I had experienced in France and in particular the food I ate in Brive. The course dealt not only with food preparation but matters that did not interest me, such as how to remove stains from pillowslips, sheets and tea towels. I attended college for about five months and I just could not take it anymore. I know that it was an excellent five-year degree course, but it was only suitable for someone who just wanted to be a hotel manager. It was, of course, an impetuous decision, but I was more interested in the preparation of food in the kitchen, so I decided to abandon the course without informing the principal, a Mr Fuller. I know that my parents were concerned that I had abandoned the course, but they said they would support me if they thought it would point me eventually in the right direction. After all, this was the second time that I had abandoned a plan for a future career—the previous project being a university place at the Sorbonne in Paris. I really had to think seriously about my future, as so far it seemed that every plan started by me with the best of intention, then came to a sudden end simply because I became bored with that particular project.

In the meantime, my sister Kitty was going out with an interesting man from Jersey with the fascinating name, Percy d'Authreau, someone she had met at the old Ritz Ballroom in St Helier while on holiday. He subsequently followed her back to Woodford on her return. He apparently had some experience in catering and many years previously was in partnership with a friend in a café called The Chick Inn in the Jersey capital. At first, he sold catering equipment and, also worked part-time in a famous pub in Chigwell called The King's Head. At this time, I was seeing quite a lot of Sandra, who had just handed in her notice at Imhofs in Oxford St.

I felt the urge to do something that would make me more responsible regarding my attitude to a project that would be a success and more permanent. When I enrolled in the Hotel School, I was automatically given a five-year temporary dispensation from doing national military service. At the time, as in most countries, it was obligatory to serve one's country from the age of eighteen for a period of two years. Quite honestly, when I abandoned the hotel course, I completely forgot that by doing so, I would still be obliged to do my national service and consequently lose my freedom for two years. The thought of my loss of freedom in an itchy uniform made me cringe and was for me beyond the pale. Quite simply, I put it out of my mind, so, therefore, the problem did not exist.

My brother Derek was a pacifist and a very gentle person who was taken to court for refusing to do his national service. Also, my father was adamant that we should not be involved in any form of violence, wars being, in his opinion, due to the incompetence of the political class. Derek appeared in court as a Conscientious Objector and must have portrayed himself as a genuine candidate for peace since the court accepted his plea. He also played an important part in the daily running of Dad's bakery, which along with other trades such as the mining industry, were invariably exempt from this military obligation. My other brother, Alan, did not go down this route. He joined the Royal Air Force, did his two years, learnt Russian and then went on to Oxford University to obtain a top-class degree with honours.

I put the idea of national service to the back of my mind. When I was at school, being in the military cadet force was obligatory from thirteen years of age, and that meant wearing a uniform once a week, which was always a Monday. I do not know whether I have an allergy to itchy clothing, but when I had to put on the hairy shirt, hairy thick and bristly trousers, a belt with flaky Blanco on it, it completely ruined my day. I told Mum about this little idiosyncrasy that bothered me, so she came up with a brilliant innovative idea. She took some beautiful silk material from one of her petticoats and sewed it into my trousers, and also lined my shirt with it. I detested Mondays at school when we also had gymnastics. After sweating profusely in the gymnasium, we could not take a shower as the only showers were some distance away within the swimming pool area, so all the boys had to clamber back, sweat and all, into the most itchy and uncomfortable clothing imaginable. So, doing two years in the army was not for me, but as I said, I put this problem to the back of my mind, so in theory, it did not exist.

Kitty's boyfriend Percy had decided to leave his job in the kitchen of the King's Head and spoke to me one evening about this decision.

"What are you going to do, Percy, because you know that my father is always suspicious of people who are unemployed?"

"Yes, I know your father's view on this subject," he replied.

As mentioned before, at that time, all over the UK, there was an enormous mushrooming of coffee bars just about everywhere. In Woodford, we had the Calypso; in Wanstead, The Bamboo Bar and in Snaresbrook, La Fiesta.

Suddenly I had an idea. I said to Percy, "Look, Percy, we have both abandoned our present obligations regarding work, so what about opening a coffee bar together?"

He immediately showed great interest in my idea. We were both aware that rents in Woodford High St were prohibitive, so we decided to look further afield to carry out our proposed plan. It was one day in 1958 we were driving in Dad's car and found ourselves in Lea Bridge Rd when we saw a lock-up shop with a 'lease for sale' notice in the window. It was situated just a few yards from a working man's café, which was always busy. But this would not affect our plan because it was just a café with a very healthy trade for lorry drivers and not the sort of place that would serve the food and the slightly more upmarket plan we envisaged, should we be successful in obtaining the lease. Percy parked the car in this café's car park and wrote down all the details displayed in the window of our prospective café. We then went into the lorry drivers' café and found a table in the corner. The proprietor served us with two cups of coffee that tasted vaguely like the contemptible liquid coffee at the time called 'Camp Coffee', which was a black liquid that came in a bottle and to which you added freshly boiled milk. The taste was awful, but at that time, the choice of instant coffee was very limited. If you wanted to have real ground coffee at home, you would need a percolator, something I had never seen at home or elsewhere. The owner was very polite and told us that the shop we were interested in had changed hands on numerous occasions with so many different trades that he doubted that anyone could ever make a success of it. This was a challenge, but at the time, we just listened to the café owner's advice and stayed silent. It was only when we got back into the car that we looked at each other and agreed that if the terms of the lease were favourable, then we should open it as a coffee bar. Percy, with his knowledge of cooking, could prepare the food, and I would serve it and also be in charge of the Gaggia coffee machine. After all, I did have a certain degree of experience serving espresso coffee at La Fiesta coffee bar when this little evening job was available for part-time students at ten shillings for four hours' work. Percy was wise and felt that I should slow down a bit. First of all, we had to make the necessary enquiries with the estate agent, which we did, and when we decided to go ahead, we contacted the lawyer who was also acting for the vendor and asked him to act for us too. There was no ingoing, so all we had to pay was the rent—£300 per annum. At the time, it seemed a lot to me, but that was for both of us one hell of a challenge because the place had to be made to look like a proper coffee bar, and that would cost money. Fortunately, Percy seemed to have an entourage of acquaintances who were also tradesmen. However, as we did not have that sort of money available, we informed them of this fact and said that bills would be paid as the money came in from the coffee shop. This was agreed, so we went ahead in making the premises as inviting as possible with the least expenditure. We managed to purchase a second-hand Gaggia coffee machine from another coffee shop that went bankrupt—that should perhaps have been a warning! Then we had the shop completely rewired. Percy and I worked very hard at painting and decorating the interior, the walls receiving two coats of emulsion paint and then a quick gloss on the skirting boards. What seemed most expensive at the time were several internal glass effigies fitted high up, above the left- hand side of our proposed counter. We then decided to come up with a Spanish name for our new venture, and it would be known as El Fandango. We managed to buy a second-hand jukebox and installed it in a prominent position next to the kitchen. In the meantime, Percy and I did our homework. Obviously, by now, I was well-known in the local coffee bars whereas Percy, being a lot older than me, preferred the casual atmosphere of the two local pubs. However, he did the rounds with me and I must say that there was a great deal of interest in our project and everybody seemed enthusiastic and encouraging regarding our plans. Promises were made that visits to El Fandango would take place, and they certainly did. As I was now seeing Sandra on a regular basis and the fact that she had abandoned her job in London, she seemed very enthusiastic about joining Percy and me and would be there to wait on tables and serve coffee. The three of us did an evening tour of all the local coffee bars, and in each one, we spoke to as many people as possible explaining our new venture and at the same time offering free coffee and snacks to those prepared to listen to us and pay us a visit. It must have worked because on opening night we were pleased to see so many young people there and, in fact, some more mature ones, who apparently had given up on a night at the local pub and honoured us with a visit. The Lea Bridge Road area did not have the same panache as Woodford Green, and at first, this was a worry that Percy and I had a great deal of concern about. However, with our opening night out of the way – and along with it a till full of coins and notes – we were both delighted, but we realised that it would not be this busy every night. We were wise enough not to get too excited, but we knew we had made a good start.

Percy was always in the kitchen, where he felt more at home, whereas Sandra served on the tables, and I was behind the counter handling and serving frothy cappuccinos and preparing the odd snack. The old jukebox churned out all the latest Cliff Richard and Elvis Presley hits, and I distinctly remember a customer in his late twenties who always played the same song by Elvis and at times looked as if he could be problematic as he was in the habit of constantly banging his fist on the glass section of the jukebox as if to keep in harmony with the song. He turned out to be harmless and explained that as a soldier in the infantry, he had just returned from Cyprus where he said he saw and did things that disgusted him. This was when Enosis was created as an anti-colonialist group to flush out the British and achieve independence.

Sandra and myself on opening night at our coffee bar "El Fandango" receiving our first bank note.

One afternoon, when business was quieter, I went next door to the newsagent to buy the *Evening Standard*. I came back and sat at a table where Sandra had just put two hot coffees. She was very good at doing and completing crossword puzzles and, in fact, boasted that she once completed the *Daily Telegraph* crossword on the train journey from Snaresbrook to Oxford Circus station, which would last on average approximately, fifty-five minutes. In the paper, there was a competition, and the idea was to answer questions correctly every night for a week and then construct a phrase that Charlie Drake (a comedian at that time) could use in his act on stage. Personally, I could not be bothered to answer any of these trivial questions and told her so, but she persisted and completed them all by the end of the week. After this, she turned to me and said, "Can you make up a phrase for Charlie Drake to use in his act?"

Without thinking, I replied, "Sorry I'm late, mate, but I just missed my queue" (play on words with cue on stage!). She duly sent off the completed coupon to the *Evening Standard,* and we never thought any more about it until my mother phoned me at the shop ten days later to say that we had won the first prize out of eight thousand people and that the editor informed my mother that part of the prize was to be collected personally from our homes in Woodford and then be driven directly to the London Palladium in a chauffeur-driven Rolls Royce, where Bruce Forsyth, Edmund Hockridge, Bernard Bresslaw, Charlie Drake and the rest of the cast were waiting to greet us. Compared to today's generous parlour games on TV, our prizes were insignificant, but part of the prize was to have a gastronomic dinner and see the cabaret at the Talk of the Town nightclub near Piccadilly. The chauffeur was waiting for us as we left the nightclub and promptly drove us home along with our prizes: nylon stockings for Sandra, £10 Premium Bonds for me and a few other trivial little gifts! The next day our photo, along with all the stars, was displayed across the front page of the *Evening Standard*. I must say that this brought in several new customers into the coffee bar. No business like show business!

Me with champagne, Bernard Bresslaw, comedian little Charlie Drake, my
future wife next to Bruce Forsyth

The reluctant soldier arrives in Jersey

Percy and I were very happy with the success of our opening night, but we both realised that this was not going to be repeated daily. Even though its main attraction was the excellent coffee that we served in a really continental atmosphere, Percy in the kitchen prepared a very simple menu, cooking food that was only basic but very tasty. Also, we got on very well with each other. We both had our own section and worked in harmony. He lived alone in the basic accommodation above the premises, and I was still living at home. We genuinely felt pleased with what we had achieved, and this continued for several months. But like everything in life, things do not always work out as planned. I was happy with having met Sandra. I was also grateful for the invaluable help she contributed to the business, and pleased that she seemed to enjoy being with me in this new venture. I remembered sitting next to her in class when we were perhaps just nine years of age in St Mary's Convent, both trembling with fear when the voice of Sister Madeline bellowed out some direct order at one of us. So, it was great to be able to retrace our steps over the past, to talk about growing up and now as adults forming a relationship. Unfortunately, this sense of permanence, security and independence that the coffee bar brought came to a sudden stop early one morning.

The previous evening was a very busy one at El Fandango—more coffees served than meals, but it was a good result with the till working overtime. I left very late that night after giving a lift to a lovely lady of a certain age who helped Percy and me wash the dishes on a part-time basis. I drove Mrs Geary home in my little Renault 750. I went back to pick up Sandra, who had been busy putting away the last of the coffee cups on top of the Gaggia machine. I then dropped her off at her house. I was extremely tired and spoke to my parents for just a few minutes before getting into bed.

The next morning, I was awakened by my father, who was shaking me ferociously and shouting.

"What's the matter, Dad?" I shouted.

"Well," he said, "they've caught up with you at last!"

"What do you mean, Dad?"

"The postman has just been," he went on, "and this registered letter is for you, and it is telling you that since you gave up your Surrey University hotel course, you are now liable to do eighteen months of national service. You are not going to do it if I have my way. Get dressed! In half an hour, I will drive you to Southampton so that you can take the ferry to Jersey. Once there, you will not have to do national service."

I felt shocked and somewhat dazed. Dad was very forthright and was determined that I should obey his plan to have me whisked away. I thought seriously about what he said. Then suddenly, the thought of being deprived of my freedom for nearly two years horrified me plus the memory of my Combined Cadet Force days came rushing back along with the itchiest shirt, tunic and trousers imaginable. At first, I wanted to rebel against Dad's advice as I did not like being told what to do, but within the hour, I changed my mind. My suitcase was packed, and I went to say goodbye to my mother, and I promised to write to her every week. Dad and I got into the car and left immediately for Southampton. I knew Jersey from an early age when brother Alan and I would spend our holidays above a restaurant, Le Rendez-vous in the centre of St Helier, that Dad had bought some years previously but which he had since disposed of. Well, obviously, I could not stay there, so all I had in my possession was the address of a former employee, Mr John Fage and his wife Lorna, who let out rooms at a reasonable price.

I arrived in St Helier early in the morning after a crossing that took, in those days, around eight hours. I already knew that Jersey was a beautiful island, but here I was under a different set of circumstances and for me, it represented a new challenge. Suddenly from being an interested partner in a successful little coffee bar, here I was in Jersey with no home or job.

Looking back, it is with great regret that I did not even say goodbye to Percy or Sandra to tell them how worried and sorry I was to leave them in the lurch and forcing them to run the business without my support. The suddenness of my hasty decision and my failure to inform Percy of my intentions still haunts me today. Everything happened so quickly that there was not enough time to inform other family members of my leaving.

I went immediately to the home of the Jersey couple who had worked for Dad. I knew them both from my previous visits. They allowed me to rent a spare room at a reasonable and fair price. Their house was centrally situated, so it was not too difficult to find a bar where I could pop in for half a pint of Mary Ann Special. There were also fish and chip takeaways not too far from the house, so I felt very much at home. The next important thing was to get a job. I bought the *Evening Post* and scoured the jobseekers page. One that attracted my attention was working in a local bakery as a van driver.

I immediately applied for the job, and when I was interviewed by the very friendly owner of Le Brun's Bakery, I explained that from previous visits, I knew St Helier well, but some of the other parishes were unknown to me, so my request was to work around St Helier which Mr Le Marquand said could be arranged. And in addition to this, I would be driving a brand-new Morris van which would be delivered the following Monday. For the first few days, another roundsman accompanied me to show me where all the *cafés*, bars and restaurants were situated so that I could deliver to them daily. Trying to ingratiate myself with the local Jersey people, I would often ask questions referring to the German occupation and how they managed in their daily lives, so I thought that this would be a good question to discuss with the pleasant petrol pump attendant when I filled my van for the first time. His answer made me feel just a little uncomfortable.

I asked, "What was life like during the occupation?"

He replied, "Which one? The German or the English?" This was in reference, I think to the many British people with considerable wealth who came to live in Jersey to avoid death duty in the UK. Or perhaps it was a slight dig at people like me and other humble seasonal workers.

The year was 1958. My boss, Mr Le Marquand, shook my hand and congratulated me on achieving this position as the main town driver and said, "You know, Graham, we, as Jersey's biggest bakery pay the highest wages. You will be paid £8 a week!" But in those days, I must admit everything was inexpensive. A pint of beer was eleven old pence a pint, a dry Martini one and threepence, a whisky slightly more expensive, and, as most people smoked, a packet of Senior Service cost one and threepence a packet, but I managed to find a brand called Flag, and they cost me a shilling for twenty. Also, in those days, the measure for spirits was the Imperial one, which made the modern measure of a fluid ounce look meagre. How often would I hear from holidaymakers the following words at the bar "Barman, I didn't order a double."

The reply was, "No, Sir, this may look like a double, but in Jersey, we serve a large Imperial measure at exactly half the price you pay in the UK."

Things have changed dramatically in recent years because it is now possible to drink cheaper in England than in Jersey, which I know has certainly affected tourism, because, in those days, visitors to the island appreciated the extremely low price of alcohol, cigarettes, tobacco, cosmetics, perfume and aftershave. A gallon of petrol was two and sixpence a gallon. This was part and parcel of Jersey's popularity with tourists, and that is without mentioning the sensational and stunning beaches and natural beauty of the island.

But Jersey has changed, and not for the better. The strength and influence of the financial sector has become too powerful because the powers-that-be fear that their upmarket bankers would resent queuing up at the Easyjet check-in desk at the Airport next to a married couple with two screaming children. The word "grockle" was often heard when bankers described working-class holidaymakers who simply required decent accommodation, simple food, respect and value for money.

To be truthful, my leaving England seemed to me to be a way of making a fresh start—again! My job was simple, but I enjoyed the work and the other people I worked with. I had decent accommodation, and everything in Jersey was a lot cheaper than in the UK. My parents must have given Sandra my address in St Helier. In those days, there were no mobile phones or internet, just an old-fashioned phone box on the corner of Great Union Rd if I wanted to phone home. A letter arrived for me, which John gave me as I was coming through the front door. As the bakery was a four-minute walk away from my lodgings, I would often park my van outside and pop in for a coffee. John and Lorna and Lorna's mother were particularly kind and always offered me a drink at all times of the day.

I recognised Sandra's writing on the envelope, so I was pleased that I had not been forgotten. She wrote that her mind was made up and that she would be on the next available boat from Southampton. Her father would be driving her down to Southampton, and then she would be on her way.

It was my day off, so I walked down to St Helier Harbour to meet her, and since this was her very first visit anywhere outside the UK, she seemed in awe as I saw her wave to me from the exit door of the bulky passenger ferry. The boat was not full as the tourist season had not yet got underway. We embraced, and as I had no means of transport outside of work, we both walked towards the town centre and finished up in a pub that was known at that time as the Cosy Corner. We drank a half-pint of draught beer each and chatted for about an hour. We then went to my lodgings, where I introduced her to John and Lorna. It may sound somewhat old-fashioned these days, but we had no intention of living together, which nowadays would be the norm. Therefore, I asked Lorna if she knew of any lady who would be prepared to share a room or small flat with Sandra. She immediately solved this problem by saying that she knew that a female relation of hers was looking for just that arrangement.

The next day Sandra answered a job advertisement in the *Evening Post* and as a qualified shorthand typist was accepted immediately as a secretary at the Summerland Clothing Company at £9 a week. So, life was good. We both had jobs and were earning money, and, as we considered that Jersey was the best place anybody could wish to be in, we settled into a way of life that was new to both of us and very exciting. The year was 1958. We enjoyed that first season so very much and at the end of the year, we returned to Woodford to spend Christmas with our respective families. I could not consider spending too much time in the UK as there was always the prospect of being called up for military service. I decided to return to Jersey as soon as possible. This happened just a few days after Sandra and I got engaged at a simple family gathering. We returned to Jersey but still lived apart. Again, this seems a strange thing to do in this modern era, but at that time, it seemed perfectly rational.

We decided to get married in Jersey. There were just our respective parents present at St Andrew's Church; brother Derek was best man and his lovely wife Pat was also present. There were just five other people in attendance, whom I did not know. In the evening, I had a long conversation with my father about my work as a delivery driver. He said that with the public-school education that he had given me, he thought that I was worthy of better things in life. I agreed with him because I then went on to tell him that every time I delivered bread, croissants, pork pies, doughnuts to guest houses in St Helier, I always asked the respective owners how many guests they could accommodate and how many they had in at the present time. I would then consult the official tourism guidebook to see how much they charged per person and then multiply the two figures together. At that point, my mind was made up. I told my father that I was interested in running my own business such as a small guest house but buying an already established one would be too expensive, so Dad came up with the idea of looking for a town property, in a good commercial position which could be converted into a viable guest house. Until this could be achieved, Sandra and I moved temporarily into a flat in St Peter's Valley.

Every so often in the late fifties and early sixties there were property auctions that took place in Jersey and were advertised in the local press. I showed my father an advert for a dilapidated property in St Helier, which would be auctioned the following day. He said he would help me financially, which I appreciated, but this would depend on getting it at the right price. On the day of the auction, I was working, so I could not attend myself, but my father did. On returning to our flat, where my parents were staying with us, I saw a glimmer of anticipation and excitement in Dad's eyes. He said that he had successfully bid the highest price for the scruffy terraced property, which I would then do my best to develop. I hugged him and gave Mum a kiss on both cheeks. Strange as it might seem, neither Dad nor I had visited the property in Don Rd, prior to the purchase, so surprises were to come later.

We obtained the key from the auctioneer, so Dad and I went along to the property to inspect what we had purchased for the first time. Naturally, for me, it was a very exciting moment. On entering, we both looked at each other without a word being spoken. I remember sometime later, we both agreed that our mutual response should have been, "God, what the hell have we done?" Floorboards were either missing or poking out at a perpendicular angle; walls were crumbling; a staircase that was wobbly and perched at a dangerous angle, and there was no electricity—just gas lighting and no other form of heating. We learnt through our lawyer that a lady in her nineties had lived there with the help of a nurse who came in every day to look after her patient. There would be a considerable amount of work to carry out before it could become habitable, let alone suitable for taking in guests on a bed-and-breakfast basis. We were recommended to a local builder who said that he could do what was needed to complete the transformation. There were only six rooms upstairs, and downstairs was worse than a neglected slum. The builder installed a hand basin in each room, plastered the walls with Seraphite, and later covered the walls with a delicate floral wallpaper and painted the skirting boards in a brilliant white gloss. All the old floorboards were replaced, and the wobbly staircase was dismantled and thrown away. The new staircase was straight and solid. It took five months to complete the transformation. We went and bought new beds, sheets, blankets and curtains, and had net and patterned curtains with a floral design fitted downstairs and in the bedrooms. We had electricity installed, along with the basic kitchen requirements, such as a cooker, a fridge, a deep freeze and a Bendix washing machine. We were ready to go. I made an appointment with my local bank manager because I needed more money to finish our project. I dressed up smartly with a navy-blue blazer, school tie and again hair with a parting on the left-hand side and smoothed down with Brylcreem. All I was offered was £500, which seems ridiculous in today's financial market. I was not happy. Also, the bank manager kept going on about road workers who were earning as much as £50 a week. I thought I would make a slight critique of this statement by saying that we all need each other in our society and that without those important road workers, he would not be able to get to his managerial position in his Jaguar without good roads to drive on.

I put an advert in the *Evening Post*, seeking people who just wanted a room only or those who may require breakfast as well. I cannot forget the name of my very first guest. Perhaps it was the name he invented: Stanley Ottolangui. I say 'invented' because he went to obtain a work permit and told the social security that his name was A. Capone!

Another guest was a Canadian gentleman who was on holiday with his wife. I took up two cups of tea to their room every day, and he would brush past me and take his cup immediately to the toilet, where he stayed as long as it took him to drink it and complete his ablutions. As we only had one toilet at that time, it was difficult for other guests who needed to use it. This gentleman did something that has never happened since. When Sandra went to clean his room, she discovered outside the door a pair of his black shoes. As this was my first week in running a guesthouse, I thought this was the normal thing to do, so I promptly took them downstairs, plastered them with Cherry Blossom shoe polish and gave them a jolly good shine. I replaced them in the same place where I found them and thought this was a normal requirement of doing this work. But this never ever happened again. And I didn't charge him for this service.

We named the guest house 'Mornington'. This was because I lived in Mornington Road in Woodford, and as a young boy, I was evacuated during the last war to a house in High Wycombe, also called 'Mornington', so it seemed obvious to me that this title would be the appropriate one for our new venture.

After some two years, the bookings improved, and I felt that we were on the right path to making a success of this challenge. There would also be a new addition to the family. Philip was our first-born child, soon to be followed by Lyndon, Alan and Jonathan in almost consecutive years.

The adjacent property came on to the market so I saw this acquisition, if I could raise the money, as a way of expanding the business as tourism at that time was the most important financial asset and flourishing. In fact, just a few years later, it was common knowledge to everyone that Jersey had, during the season, the second-busiest airport in the UK, Heathrow being the number one. A plane took off or landed every three minutes in Jersey. For the average British person, Jersey was like going abroad without the need for passports, foreign money, food difficulties and the fear of speaking a foreign language.

I managed to buy the adjoining property but could not incorporate it into the guest house as I bought it with sitting tenants who rightly had to be protected for a period of three years before I could obtain vacant possession. Therefore, any plans for expansion were put on hold. However, I succeeded in getting plans passed to add three more bedrooms to the existing roof area, which would then give us a total of twenty-one licensed guests. I then applied to the Licensing Bench to obtain a residential licence to serve alcoholic drinks from a minuscule bar that a local carpenter had constructed for me. This was neatly fitted in the corner of our dining room. The only character reference I could produce to show the Bailiff in his chambers was my German master's very pleasant handwritten letter. Sir Robert Masurier was the Bailiff at that time and, peering over his glasses, said, "Isn't the applicant of a slightly immature age?" This was directed at my advocate, Mr Peter Giffard, who replied quite curtly, "Your Honour, better to have youth on one's side than senility!"

The Bailiff smiled gently, and I received his approval. Mr Giffard told me later that at that time, I was the youngest person ever to hold a drinks licence.

During this period, Jersey was a great success story from the point of view of tourism. Farming was also a success—in particular, for the famous potato and tomato crops that were considered to be the best in the world, along with milk, butter, and dairy produce. The finance sector was becoming more important and eventually developed into what it is today, with its tax-haven status renowned all over the world.

*   *   *   *

Over the next few years, I managed to incorporate all the adjoining properties into the original Mornington so that we eventually could accommodate nearly seventy guests. It involved five properties in total, which meant an enormous financial commitment to purchase them in the first place and then to carry out the necessary alterations to bring them up to modern hotel standards. Such an outlay was a financial headache, but with the popularity of Jersey at that time increasing and it becoming the number-one choice of holidaymakers, we could have let another ten rooms to capacity, such was the demand for accommodation. Each room had its own modern private bathroom, wide-screen TV, tea- and coffee-making facility, and everything to make a prospective guest appreciate their stay with us.

Before we had the rooms modernised, my mind went back to the days when we just had washbasins in each one. Our young waitress-cum-chambermaid rushed into the kitchen as I was blanching chips to tell me that she could not clean one of the rooms where there were two sisters and a young child. She tried to explain, looking very embarrassed, that there was something in the waste-paper bin but blushed and could not tell me what it was, so I went upstairs to this family room on the first floor. I knocked on the door and was greeted by two attractive ladies with a heavy Cockney accent.

"Mornin' love!" they both shouted as one of them opened the door. I could not help but notice the little boy crouched, with pants down, balancing precariously on the waste-paper bin. He was doing what comes naturally to a little boy of that age. I then realised why my chambermaid was reluctant to tell me what she saw in the bin. "Madam," I started, "why is your boy using the bin as a toilet?"

She replied, "Sorry, mate. I fought that is what the bleedin' thing was for."

"No, it is not! There is a toilet just along the corridor, so in future, please use this facility for your little boy and now would you kindly retrieve what your son has left in the bin and take it to the toilet?"

Having a Residential drinks licence at such a very immature age made me realise how fortunate I was to be in such a privileged position, not wanting ever to commit some misdemeanour and risk losing it. We had a booking that came from a family who lived in West Ham. The couple arrived with their son Robert, who was about sixteen years of age. I showed them to their respective rooms and explained to them at what time we served breakfast and the evening meal. They were very friendly and could not stop talking about their local football team, West Ham and especially their praise in extoling the virtues, leadership and ability of their Captain Bobby Moore.

What happened next, I put down to my desire to cherish and preserve my position as the youngest licensee in Jersey and uphold the principles and obligations that went hand-in hand with that title. At the age of thirteen my mother encouraged me to be confirmed in St Paul's Cathedral, along with other pupils from my school. I think she meant well and thought it would give me a moral stance and high standards during my developing years. I believe she thought it would help instil in me ecclesiastical and moral principles, but thankfully that never happened. I went into the bar and had a drink with the family from West Ham and once more they spoke about their club and how they won the World Cup in 1966 repeating time and time again the names of Bobby Moore, Geoff Hurst and Martin Peters. It was a particularly hot day in Jersey and far too hot for them, so they decided to have an early night and went to their room. Their son, Robert stayed behind and started talking to the daughter of a couple from Birmingham. She was also about sixteen years of age. I could see this young couple were deep in conversation and they seemed to be getting on well with each-other. Perhaps it was the combination of my mother's desire to instil in me these puritanical views and my wish not to endanger my drinks licence. I look back in horror at what I did next. I suddenly realised that the young couple were no longer in the bar. I also knew that the West Ham supporting parents were already in their room, so I felt morally responsible for what eventuality was about to take place on my premises.

After about ten minutes and having just served a guest with a Martini, I became concerned about this young couple and their sudden disappearance from the bar. In those days we had no lift so I scooted up three-flights of stairs, seemingly as fast as Roger Bannister's four-minute mile and arrived out of breath in front of Robert's room. I hammered on the door and shouted "Robert, are you in there with that young lady?" It took him some time to answer me. "Yes she is," was his out of breath response.

I shouted "This is not a glorified brothel, I do not expect this sort of behaviour in my establishment". The girl came to the door, looking somewhat dishevelled and ran her fingers through her hair. She then disappeared to her room on the first floor. How could I have done such a thing? Thankfully things have changed so much since those days of artificial, superfluous and pathetic moral principles. Now for the good news!

However, Robert, the sixteen-year-old boy at the time is now a fully grown family man of 75 years of age who still regularly comes to the hotel. Every year in the bar he encourages me to repeat to other guests exactly what happened to him all those years ago, which I now describe in florid and slightly exaggerated terms and at the same time expressing my shame that has now given way to light comic relief every time new guests listen to this story. He said the reason why it took him so long to open the bedroom door was his fumbling effort in trying to get dressed quickly and that he inadvertently kept putting both feet into the same trouser leg. It was also his very first attempt in the art of seduction. At the time I promised him that I would not tell his parents as to what actually happened that night. I kept my promise.

On another occasion, we had a man who occupied a double room with his wife and stayed with us for two weeks. He always wore a suit, collar and tie and looked well-dressed, but there was a slight odour if he came too close to me. Chambermaids do have the habit of talking about their rooms and those who occupy them. For instance, how many empty bottles of wine, gin or whisky they have to throw in the glass-bin or on another occasion when they were making the bed and found a vibrator under the pillow. However, the room containing the man in the suit was proof that all hygienic standards were not being fully met. The chambermaid told me that for the last two weeks, she did not once have to clean the shower tray or tiles. I was absolutely shocked that two people could spend two weeks in the bedroom, and not once did either of them use this facility. This same man, a few years later, made a reservation for one week only, but this time he was not with the original lady. I made no comment and, as discreetly as possible, gave him a key to a different room to the one he had previously occupied with his wife, which I thought was diplomatic. A few minutes later, he came to reception slightly flustered, saying that he expected to have the same room as before. Fortunately, this room was available, so I gave him the key, and he went happily upstairs to the very room he occupied on the previous occasion with his first lady. He still wore the same suit, collar and tie and had the same smell about him, but I hesitated to ask the chambermaid whether or not there was prevalent use of the shower during his stay with us.

Being a licensee, I was always aware of the residual behaviour that follows a session involving excess drinking of alcohol. Late into the evening, I was behind the bar serving customers when I heard an unusual noise in reception. I rushed out and saw two men physically holding up and supporting one of my guests, who was totally unable to stand up. I told them that the drunk man could not come into the bar, so they should take him immediately to his room and put him to bed. After a few minutes, the two men came down and politely asked permission to have a drink. They said he was now in his room, and from what they believed he had consumed, they thought that he would not be down for breakfast. This little problem seemed to have been resolved, but as we shall see later, not really.

In the days following the transformation of the former guest house into a hotel, we had a policy of including morning tea in the tariff so everybody would have a cup of tea delivered by a waitress and me to each room. I have always been a little bit fanatical regarding serving piping-hot tea to the rooms, and that meant warming the pot and the cups, adding the loose tea and allowing the brew to stand for two minutes before pouring it through a strainer into each cup and delivering it as quickly as possible to the guest bedrooms. I was always accompanied by the waitress on duty. I would knock on the door three times; she would open it. I would pass the cups of tea to her, then she would enter the room and place the cups on the bedside table. However, on this occasion, there was something blocking the door; it just would not open. So, as I am very precise about serving piping-hot tea, I told the waitress that we had to move on and go along the corridor to deliver the rest of the tea to the other rooms. When this was completed, we returned to the first room to see if the door was now unwedged. I told the waitress to go down to the kitchen to make a fresh cup of tea for the occupant of the room whose door was still jammed. Despite my knocking, nobody came to the door. I checked the register and found out that this room was the one occupied by the man who was very drunk the night before. I simply put my shoulder hard against the door to create a small gap around the frame. I could see that he was not in bed—in fact, it was still made-up and not slept in. I then squeezed my head around the door and was totally shocked when I saw a stiff, motionless body stretched out on the floor. It was the first time in my life that I had seen a dead body. The waitress, in the meantime, appeared with a fresh cup of tea, which I automatically drank. The waitress screamed. I called the emergency services, and they arrived a few minutes later to confirm that our guest was dead. In those days, the reception and dining room were open-plan, so after the police and emergency personnel had completed their investigation into his death, they had to carry the stretcher past the guests who were sitting down ready for their breakfast. All the guests could see the body being put into the ambulance. "Does this happen very often?" a man asked me.

Before I could answer, the man sharing his table said, "It must be the pork sausages!"

We had a charming little waitress from Newcastle, Carole, who was a hard worker and also had an affable disposition and a good sense of humour. One evening, just before serving dinner, I noticed that she had been to the hairdressers, and I complimented her saying how pretty she looked with the new style. Service was very rapid because British people do not like waiting long when they are hungry. On this occasion, Carole's demeanour had changed dramatically. She returned to the kitchen in tears. She said she had just served a couple near the fire door, and when asked by the husband how much she paid for her hairdo, she told him, and the man replied, "I wouldn't fucking well pay that price for my missus' hairdo!"

I was furious because I cannot accept bad language, especially to a lady, so I left the kitchen and went straight up to the table and spoke to the man.

"In this hotel, we give respect to all our guests and do not tolerate bad language. We expect the same in return!"

The dining room was packed, but suddenly, there was silence. For a moment, I thought that the wife of the man with the offensive tongue was being conciliatory and helpful because she looked at me with an understanding and sympathetic glance and said, "Pet, don't be upset with him, because even at home he's always fucking swearing."

I raised my eyes in disbelief and returned to my kitchen.

On another occasion, we received a mixed school party, along with four teachers. One of the waitresses rushed into the kitchen to tell me that the children were throwing my beautiful trifle at each other and that there was total pandemonium in the dining room. As

I entered the dining room, the unruly pupils were still throwing trifle around the room, and as I looked for culprits of this trifle-throwing competition, I received a custard sponge full in my face. I went over to the suspect table and said, "Stand up, the boy who threw this trifle at me!" Absolute silence, so I went up to the table where the teachers were sitting, and as I was wiping away the trifle from my face, I said to them, "You have totally lost control of your pupils. All of you are a disgrace to the teaching profession!"

Every situation does often have its funny moments, I suppose, and, in this case, someone shouted, "Speak up; I can't hear you."

I heard a voice saying, "He must be a trifle deaf."

Bergerac Arrives

The bar was always busy because not only was the price cheaper than most pubs, but there was a cosy atmosphere that guests appreciated. There were weeks when all the guests knew each other from previous visits, and throughout the year, they would all keep in contact with each other and arrange to be at the hotel for the same period every year. One such couple, Stan and Helen Coldham and daughter Jackie, celebrated twenty-five consecutive years with us, so to show our appreciation and gratitude for such loyalty, we were very lucky in successfully asking John Nettles of Bergerac fame, to come along and present a silver ornament to the family. Needless to say, when the Jersey detective walked into the bar, there was absolute pandemonium, with guests stamping their feet, cheering and women, in particular, rushing up to him for his autograph and for the odd kiss on the cheek. Stan gave a speech saying that he was suspicious that something was afoot from the moment he was met at the Jersey Airport by a luxurious chauffeur-driven limousine, which I had arranged with a local taxi company. "But," he continued, "I didn't expect to spend an evening with the most famous detective in Jersey!"

Mr and Mrs Stan Coldham being presented by John Nettles with a silver plaque celebrating 25 consecutive years at the Mornington.

Guests Behaving Badly

One memorable evening was a visit from the band of the Royal Marines, who stayed with us on several occasions. The beautiful Howard Davis Park being opposite the hotel was the obvious reason why they wished to be close to where they would be playing. They had two performances a day, playing to packed and enthusiastic audiences. After one evening performance, they all trooped back to the bar full of the joys of spring – but this was summer – and I could tell that it was going to be a busy night. Drink after drink, they came up to be served at the bar, so I knew that it was going to be difficult to close by one o'clock in the morning. There was a great atmosphere amongst the sixty or more people that night. I had a very good barman, Mark from Scotland, who really excelled at his job with speedy service and at the same time keeping the guests amused with his own specific brand of humour. I served a tall, fair-haired man with a pint of lager and noticed that he still had another unfinished glass on the counter. He was very quiet and seemed to distance himself from the other members of the band. As I had not seen him before, because most of my time was spent in the kitchen, I asked him his room number. He replied, "Number 84." I knew immediately something was wrong because the hotel only had thirty-one rooms. As each guest is automatically supplied with a secret front-door code to gain access to the hotel, I assumed this man must have crept in while genuine guests were using the entrance code. I then explained to this man that under my strict residential licence rule, it was a licence for residents only.

"Well then, what are you going to do about it?" he growled.

I replied, "I am requesting you to leave the premises." I took away the recently poured pint of lager, which was on the counter and said to him, "I shall come to the other side of the counter to reimburse you for your pint of lager."

In the meantime, to kill time, I cleaned all the ashtrays and passed them to Mark so that he could put them back on the tables and counter. I stood next to the blonde stranger and asked Mark to pass me the money for the pint of lager I took away from him.

"You took away my pint!" the blonde man shouted at me.

"Yes, I did and here is the money for your pint," I replied, "I am asking you politely to leave as you are not resident in this hotel."

The bar, being packed solidly with the band members, suddenly became silent; everybody heard the man's loud voice shouting at me, and I remember distinctly that as I spoke to him face to face, the juke box was playing the last few bars of Noel Harrison's 'Windmills of your Mind'. In all the years I've had the bar, I had never witnessed such an atmosphere of potential violence that I experienced that night. The bar was packed, the jukebox was silent, and the onlookers were waiting in anticipation for the next move. The blonde man, with his nose almost touching mine, said, "We'll sort this out, outside where I am going to knock your fucking head in."

I put both my arms down by my side so that I would not show any aggressive behaviour towards him and looked him in the face. Very calmly and slowly, I replied, "Look, let me tell you something about Jersey law. If you hit a licensee, it is the same as hitting a policeman. That means that you will automatically go inside for at least six months. Now, as you can see, I have my hands down by my side, and in this bar, you have about sixty witnesses. So, I think there is no need to think about going outside because if you are going to be violent towards me, I would like as many people as possible to witness such a scene."

You could hear the proverbial pin drop. Not a word was spoken. Everybody was waiting for the next move. It came from him. He simply put his empty glass back on the counter and slowly walked away to leave by the front door. I was surprised and flattered by what happened next. All sixty guests broke out in simultaneous applause, and several of them came up to me to congratulate me on the way I handled this sensitive situation. I really did not expect this, and I felt relieved but slightly embarrassed. One man, before going up to his room, said, "See you in the morning Dr Kissinger."

Just to the side of my kitchen was the flat I lived in, as being close to my place of work was of the utmost importance. I must say, on looking back, that it was a very confined area for a married couple with four children, but as with most seasonal businesses, we sacrificed a great deal of our domestic privacy, knowing that with closure at the end of the season we would have a choice of rooms upstairs, where the boys would have more room to play.

One evening, Mark rushed into the flat to tell me that a man was using bad language in the bar. This is something I have never come to terms with as swearing is above all unacceptable, whether carried out in front of a lady or amongst men. It is just a weakness I find unacceptable and abominable. "Mark," I replied, "tell me where the man is situated in the bar, describe him to me, how he is dressed, and I will be through to sort him out."

Mark said he was tall, bald and wearing a blazer. As I entered the bar, I could see that Mark was changing a barrel of lager in the little room adjacent to the bar, out of sight of the customers. I went straight up to the tall, bald man with a blazer, who was leaning against the bar with a pint in his hand. I said, "If you ever use foul and disgusting language in my hotel again, you not only will not be served, but I will oblige you to leave this establishment."

While I was laying down the law to this recalcitrant individual, I noticed out of the corner of my eye that Mark was waving his arms furiously with a pained look on his face. "You've got the wrong man Graham, the real culprit is sitting over there!"

Oh my God! I was so apologetic to this innocent gentleman who was very understanding, as he too had heard the tirade of bad language himself. I told Mark to serve him and his wife with complimentary drinks all night. The real culprit sitting in the corner was also tall, bald and wearing a blazer and saw me coming towards him and put out a conciliatory hand towards me. He had heard my every word and did not need a verbal lecture. As it happened, he turned out to be a nicer person than previously envisaged and full of apologies.

I think that alcohol, if used sensibly, can be a relaxing part of daily life, but as a licensee, I have seen the suffering both domestically and commercially that it can cause. In the reception area, I had a beige Victoriana chaise-longue which I adored. I made sure that every day one of the chambermaids would scrupulously clean it to perfection. One evening as I was about to close the bar, I saw a man in a suit curled up and stretched out on my chaise-longue with his grubby shoes perched on the plush wooden and velvet arm rest. I instinctively knew, right away, that he was not a resident. As so often happens, he must have gained entry when another guest with the secret code entered and he must have slipped through unnoticed. To make this little episode clearer, I must point out that at the time, I had a moustache and very dark, wavy hair which is now white with the passage of time and often, I had been taken for someone not appearing to be English. I tapped this man on the shoulder, which half-woke him up, and I could smell whisky on his breath as his eyes rolled around in a circular direction. "You are not resident in this hotel. Would you kindly leave? If you do not, I will have to call the police."

He could hardly stand up, and as he just about managed to put two wobbly legs together, he shouted at me, "Don't you tell me what to do, I fought against you fucking Italian wops during the last war!" I opened the front door, and somehow, he managed to walk with great difficulty towards it and then disappeared into the road outside. I gave the chaise-longue a good clean before going to bed. People's behaviour really does shock me, especially after an excess of alcohol. It totally changes a person who is normally soft, gentle and courteous into one of harshness, belligerence and very rude behaviour. But that is just a small part of the routine of running a hotel because, for the most part, the guests are charming, kind and respectful. Unfortunately, it is the bad behaviour of the few that spoils the holiday for the majority. Our hotel was certainly not one that could be called upmarket because it was comfortable as opposed to luxurious and reasonably priced, which appealed to a decent and appreciative section of the public.

Some time later, we had a party of men staying with us for a long weekend to celebrate a bachelor's last taste of freedom from prospective marital bliss. At the same time, there was a young couple who came to the island not only to spend time together but to get engaged. At that time in Jersey, every luxury item, whether it be a car, perfume, alcohol, tobacco and jewellery were so reasonably priced – often at half the price of the UK – that it encouraged people to come to the island, not just to have an enjoyable holiday but to take advantage of inexpensive products found everywhere in all the shops. The atmosphere in the bar was electric, with everybody talking so loudly that it was almost impossible to hear Charles Aznavour singing '*Hier Encore*' from the jukebox when the young couple walked in and made their way to sit on two of the high stools around the bar. There was so much noise with all the chattering and the loud music that the young man asked me to turn down the jukebox because he wanted to make an announcement. Suddenly, there was silence. The young man spoke softly and said that he had come to Jersey for a special reason and that was to get engaged. From his pocket, he produced a little velvet box. He opened it, took out a little diamond ring and put it on his prospective fiancée's finger, and said, "Will you marry me, darling?"

"Yes, of course I will," she replied and promptly took hold of his hand very tightly and kissed him on the lips. All the men at the bachelor party congratulated the couple with handshakes for the man and kisses on the cheek for the lady. Everybody was celebrating this romantic moment, and drinks were flowing in all directions. I noticed the young couple were drinking excessively, and as so often happens, this leads to arguments. Voices were raised, and just before midnight, I heard him shouting at his fiancée, telling her to "Get lost, I've had enough, I'm off to bed". Just for a moment, the bar went quiet because two of our other customers, noticeably women of a certain age, went up to the young girl to offer their commiseration. One of them said, "Darling don't you think you should go up to your room to be with him?"

She replied, "No, I just want another drink." I called last orders around midnight because, as usual, I had a six-thirty start in the morning to prepare the cooked breakfast. The girl had a last drink, as did the men at the bachelor party, so I managed to close the bar and leave everybody in reception, where some of them were finishing their drinks. I noticed that the recently engaged girl had not gone upstairs to join her fiancé but was talking in a lively way to the party of men.

However, I was very tired, and before going to bed, I was in the habit of pouring myself a small dry Martini with a zest of lemon and some crushed ice, listening to Carole King singing 'You've got a friend'. It was good not having to talk to anyone but just to sit in my flat in silence. I finished my drink and was just about to get into bed when I heard a repetitive noise coming from the laundry room. I had for years been meaning to replace the old faithful Bendix washing machine, but I think it was finally on its last legs because when it got to the final spinning process, it made one hell of a grating and screeching noise. We do at times allow guests to use this laundry facility, but I should have upgraded the machine years ago. However, always thinking of my guests' comfort, I got out of bed to do something about the incessant thumping noise and thought I should go and turn off the machine. As a security measure, for staff and guests alike, there was a small light that came on automatically at night and gave just enough clarity so that nobody would stumble in the dark. My flat was adjacent to the laundry room so when I went towards it to turn off the washing machine, I could not believe what I saw. The girl who had just got engaged was in a compromising position leaning forward against the washing machine with both arms outstretched for support and physically enjoying the company of one of the men from the bachelor party who was standing behind her and obviously having the time of his life.

The next morning the recently engaged couple came down for breakfast, the girl seemed very happy; she and her fiancé appeared to have made up their differences and were holding hands across the table. I often wonder whether or not they are still together.

We had a middle-aged French couple staying on a bed and breakfast basis because eating dinner at six-thirty in the evening would be out of the question for them, being far too early. However, they did enjoy their aperitif at the same time every evening, while the English were having their meal. As we were about to serve dinner, our other barman Peter came to me in the kitchen to tell me that the French couple would like to speak to me. I said I would go into the bar to see them after dinner had been served. Later I went to see them in the bar, and they had what I can only call a very wry smile on their faces. They could not speak a word of English, so we spoke in French.

"Je voudrais bien que vous m'expliquiez quelque chose, Monsieur."

"Yes, of course I will answer your question and explain things to you."

They wanted to know more about the social and drinking habits of the English because the man said he had just seen something that would cause a mini-revolution in French gastronomy. Apparently, while they were having their aperitif, two Englishmen came into the bar before dinner and drank two brandies, then they ordered two pints of lager to drink with their dinner and then after they had eaten they came back into the bar and ordered two Pastis. I had to agree and sympathise with their shock at seeing someone doing everything in reverse order. *"Ah, mon Dieu, les Anglais!"* he said with both hands on his head and laughing heartily.

I was at reception making out a bill for an extremely polite young man. I gave him the bill, and suddenly he blushed and nervously said that he had not ordered nor eaten the two rounds of ham sandwiches I had mistakenly put on his bill. I apologised for my error, but he went on to say he still would not mind paying for them, thinking it may otherwise mess up my end of the day balance sheet. This just goes to prove that there really are so many decent people who are kind and considerate. I assured him that it was my mistake and that he was not going to pay for someone else's sandwiches.

A few days later, we had an enquiry from a travel agent asking for a single room for one gentleman who would be coming to Jersey to play snooker. When he arrived at reception, I immediately recognised him from his television appearances: it was Alex Higgins. He was accompanied by a man who was his sponsor for the exhibition snooker that Mr Higgins would be playing in the island. At first, I was slightly apprehensive about his being with us as often a celebrity's reputation can cause concern, especially when there are other paying guests to consider. However, I must say that his behaviour was impeccable. He and his entourage of friends were excellent drinkers, and his entire stay went without incident.

*   *   *   *

It is strange how one's fixed views, whether on political or social matters, can be changed by circumstance. Having been brought up in a family where capital punishment was an acceptable form of punishment for a murder committed, it would need a total reversal of my family values and principles to push me into another direction. A guest was responsible for my change of view regarding retribution. We had a guest who stayed with us during the winter for five weeks, so I managed to get to know him reasonably well. We used to drink together in the bar, and on several occasions, we would go to a pub near the beach where there was a bar billiard table. We did this several times, and I judged him to be a decent man. He left the hotel, and I heard nothing more from him. A few weeks later, I picked up the local newspaper to learn that he had stabbed a woman to death in a fit of jealous rage. As a result, I always have, since that moment, endeavoured to see the best in people and tried to understand their motives and not to criticise their inability to function as a normal citizen, irrespective of the abominable act of such a heinous crime.

Looking back over the years, regarding punishment and retribution, it was around 1962 when another violent act took place. A merchant ship docked in St Helier harbour, and a young cabin boy of eighteen years of age got off the boat to walk into St Helier to see where the shops were. He had only walked a hundred yards or so when he saw a car parked with the key visible in the ignition. He got inside, drove about fifty yards and crashed the car against one of the bollards. He was immediately arrested, taken to the police court, which was still in session and was immediately sentenced by the judge to six strokes of the birch, which in those days was legal. After his thrashing, he was escorted back to his ship, where he was forced to stay until the boat left the following day. Fortunately, this cannot happen now as the law forbids such a violent punishment.

*   *   *   *

We dealt with a local laundry firm for most of the bedding, sheets and pillowcases, but there were times when we received young school parties one after the other on a one- or two-day stay basis, so we had the temperamental Bendix washing machine as a back-up for such a quick turnaround. Invariably a completely new intake of students could be arriving at reception before the previous party would have left. These were excellent bookings but at a very economic and affordable tariff. One particular day, as the departing young students were leaving, and fifty or more other very young pupils were arriving along with half a dozen teachers, the laundry lady rushed into my kitchen to tell me that my cursed spin dryer refused to spin. At that time, helping me run the hotel was a hard-working and charming married couple, John and Pauline. Their help was invaluable, and I shall always be grateful for their dedication and support over the years. I called John and explained that we just had nearly sixty arrivals and both machines in the laundry had broken down, so we had no dry sheets or pillowcases. I thought carefully for a moment. John suggested contacting a nearby hotel to see if they could help. Maybe it was my pride, but I thanked John for this idea, and I came up with an alternative solution. We had to make a decision. John told me that there were only twelve clean and ironed sheets available and twelve pillowslips. It suddenly came to me—an idea that, on looking back, I feel a certain shame and embarrassment, but as the proverbial expression says, the show must go on.

"Right John, top priority must be given to the teachers' accommodation, and that means they will have the sparkling clean sheets and pillowslips, and as for the children, I have a practical solution. The previous party of children, all about twelve years of age, have only spent a single night in their beds, so their sheets cannot be too soiled. These are desperate times, so we are going to do something I am very reluctant to do, but on this one occasion, it has to work, although it is something that we must never do again. Follow me into the kitchen."

From a cupboard under the stairs, I took out an ironing board and an empty spray canister, which I filled with a generous slug of my Old Spice aftershave. We were joined by Pauline, who came along with us upstairs to help prepare the rooms that were going to be occupied by the very young children. Then we started our work. To the aftershave, I added five times the amount of tap water, shook the canister and sprayed it all over the sheets—top and bottom. John plugged in the iron, and after a few minutes following my spraying efforts, Pauline took the iron to flatten the bottom sheet, the pillowslips and finally the top sheet and what with the beautiful fragrant smell, I can honestly say that I have never seen bedsheets look so spick and span. The problem was solved, and the school party had a great time with us and actually returned a year later— this time, they had proper sheets.

In my kitchen, I employed a Frenchman named Robert from Mantes-la Jolie. He was a man of great intellect whose work in the kitchen was greatly appreciated. He was really worthy of a more intellectual position in life but how he came to be working for me was interesting. Originally, we received a booking for five French people, amongst whom was Robert. For them, it was a long weekend away from Paris, but the main reason for their being at the hotel was the plight of Robert. A man of impeccable manners and sincerity, he owned a bicycle shop in France and, along with his wife, employed a team of six members of staff. Even though it was a very successful business, I can only say that a disruptive force and a break-up within his domestic relationship shocked him so much that he was unable to continue with his commercial venture, and this resulted in his losing faith in human nature and people in general, following which, he had a nervous breakdown. He suffered deep depression, and therefore, his friends said he needed a clean break, so they brought him to Jersey for that long weekend. On his return to France, he contacted me and said that he would even wash dishes if requested. I offered him a job in my kitchen, and in fact, that is exactly what he did. Having remarried, he is now retired from his business of running several guest houses and has finally found the domestic happiness that eluded him in France. When he was in the depths of depression, he would repeat the following sentence, always with a tear in his eyes, *"J'ai perdu ma femme, mes enfants et mon business, mais je n'ai jamais perdu ma dignité."* He said after losing everything of importance in life, he has still retained his dignity.

A married couple from Brittany checked in for a three-night stay. The majority of French guests prefer room and breakfast only as this allows them to sample the very good choice of nearby restaurants along with the culinary and cultural differences they offer, whether it is French, Portuguese, Spanish or Italian. Their stay was uneventful except for their day of departure. They came to reception to pay their bill and, very foolishly, I forgot to take their key and place it on the special key-rack in the office ready to hand over to the incoming guests who were due to arrive a short time after the couple's departure. This was around lunchtime. In the meantime, their bedroom had been stripped and thoroughly cleaned, ready for the arrival of the next guests. The new guests duly arrived as expected, but I could not find the key behind reception. I looked everywhere for the key, and then I looked at the guests' keyboard and realised that for the first time I had not put it in its usual place. However, I was pleased that I was able to pass over the key to the recently arrived couple. I showed them to the lift and wished them a happy stay. Back in reception, I was with John going through some of the diet requests from a table of vegetarians. To my horror, I saw the faces of the new arrivals, the husband's face red with anger shouting at me, "I didn't come here to book a room with shit spread over the towels!"

I accompanied the man to his room and saw a perfectly made-up room, but to my utter dismay I saw that across the bath was a towel caked in excrement. I apologised profusely, but understandably, he was fuming with rage as we joined his wife in reception. I told them that in all the years I had been running the hotel, nothing of this kind had ever happened before.

"Please accept my apologies, and we shall put you into a different room with a four-poster bed. They reluctantly agreed. I was concerned because they could easily have left and spread the news about this unforgivable calamity. John rushed up to their new room along with a bottle of Moët et Chandon champagne and two crystal glasses.

One of the chambermaids told me that after paying his bill, the Frenchman was seen rushing along the corridor leading to his room, so she assumed that he must have left something behind—which is an understatement because that is exactly what he did! So after settling his bill and leaving a large suitcase in reception, he then must have taken the key off the board, gone to his former room, used the toilet and wiped his backside on a towel which he left on the side of the bath. I repeatedly apologised to this couple for this disastrous start to their holiday, and in all honesty, they turned out to be a very kind and understanding couple. From that moment onwards, I was fanatical about removing the key from the guest keyboard the moment the bill was paid and placing it in its special place behind reception.

On another occasion, we had a coach party of twenty-five guests staying with us. On their departure, I said to the driver, "Do not move an inch until I check the keyboard."

Lost keys are anathema to all hoteliers. I looked at the board and found six keys missing. I know some selfish people like to keep them as souvenirs, but most people do it unintentionally, so I jumped on the coach, apologised for the delay and collected the six missing keys. They were all genuinely apologetic. I told them it was nothing and wished them a happy journey. I told the driver that he could now leave for the airport.

Considering Jersey is so close to France – about an hour and twenty minutes on the ferry – I am often surprised how few guests take the opportunity of travelling there on the Condor Service. After all, in next to no time, you can be in St Malo, which is a beautiful and historic town with an abundance of top-class restaurants, *crêperies*, *cafés*, bars, boutiques and a selection of seafood outlets as superb as anywhere in the world. It is in the Intramuros part of St Malo where all these delights await the visitor. Whenever our guests have decided to book a day trip to St Malo with us, a certain number of them come to me with an unusual request that shocked me when it happened the first time, but which I have now got used to. "We've booked to go to St Malo tomorrow, so could we pay extra and have a packed lunch?"

The very first time I heard this, I was flabbergasted. I replied, "Please forgive me for saying so, but where you are both going tomorrow, the restaurants produce possibly the finest selection and quality of seafood anywhere in the world. There are oysters from Cancale, mussels and lobsters from Cotentin in Normandy, and most important of all for meat-eaters, you have the *'pré-salé'* lamb from Mont St Michel."

I explained to my guests the process of *'pré-salé'* lamb to make it more enticing for them. I explained that in Normandy, the farmers take their sheep on to the beach at low tide where the grass has been soaked by the salt water that the receding tide has just left behind – hence the word *'pré-salé'*, meaning pre-salted – which gives the meat a unique flavour.

"No thank you, but I've never been keen on that sort of food, so if you could make us two rounds of cheese and tomato sandwiches each, an apple each and a bag of crisps we can then find a bench seat somewhere and people watch."

"But there is also the exotic Grand Aquarium with over six hundred different species of marine life that you could visit in St Malo," I added.

"No; very kind of you, but that is not our cup of tea, but talking of tea," they continued, "do you have a flask of tea that we could take with us?"

"Yes, of course I could arrange that but the coffee in St Malo isn't bad either," I replied.

One of the local customers who frequented our bar was someone who himself told a rather amusing story about people and their eating habits. A local bar had a thrift club to which the members contributed a regular few pounds each week so that there would be a big payout at Christmas. This was obviously a clever way to encourage regular drinkers to participate every week and at the same time helped to boost trade for those who just wanted to pay into the thrift club. Every year the organiser would often find that there was an excess of funds in the kitty after having paid out all the members, so he suggested that with all this extra money left over in the kitty, all forty-two members could have a one-night stay in a reasonably-priced hotel in Dinan in France. Included would be a fixed-price menu agreed by everybody. The main dish would be *'magret de canard'* (fillet of duck). They all left for France on the ferry and found the hotel simple, clean and reasonably priced and within walking distance of shops and bars. With the exception of two people who preferred chicken, everybody seemed happy with the choice of duck. Incidentally, the wine, by the carafe, was included in the price.

Now *'magret de canard'* is a delightful piece of duck breast if cooked correctly, and that means the fat side has to be criss-crossed with the blade of a sharp knife and cooked in a pan without butter or oil, as there is already so much fat content in the duck. The pan must be searing hot and, starting with the fat side down, it must have exactly five minutes on each side. Keeping up that intense heat one then adds seasoning of salt and pepper and optional *'Herbes de Provence'*. Then it must rest for five minutes before being cut into thick slices and served with a delicate light sauce with an added squeeze of orange juice. Most important of all, it has to be served pink in the centre. The piping-hot 'skillet' pan assures the customer that there will be no trickles of blood on the plate, but the middle will be sealed to perfection. When the duck arrived at the two long trestle tables for forty-two diners, there was silence, no comment, no emotion.

"Je vous souhaite bon appétit et bonne continuation," said the waitress.

"I cannot eat raw meat," said one man.

"Neither can I," said another.

Apart from the two people who ordered chicken, thirty-seven people returned their plates and asked the waitress in English for the chef to 'cook the meat properly'. The chef was horrified. He had to re-cook the fillets of duck until they had completely lost their correct pink texture and had been assassinated. My informant told me that after the meal had been eaten, he saw the chef talking to some French diners at a nearby table and heard the following words, as he raised his hands in a surrender position above his head, eyes gazing towards the ceiling, lips pursed, *"Ah les Anglais, c'est toujours la même chose chez eux!"* In fact, not wishing to denigrate further the British attitude as to how food in France should be cooked, it is a well-known fact with French chefs that the English in particular like their meat either overcooked *(bien cuit)* or just medium *(à point)*. Over the years working in France, I know from personal experience that when a waitress returns to the kitchen with the order, saying "four well-done steaks" for table 5, the chef will automatically shout, *"Ah nous avons des Anglais chez nous ce soir!"*

In my hotel, I had a similar experience. With lamb and beef, I deliberately endeavour to cook joints in such a way that even though I know the meat should remain pink in the centre, I still just slightly overcook it to keep our British clients happy. On this particular occasion, we had a sprinkling of mixed nationalities, so I had to try to succumb to each nation's individual preferences, so I undercooked a beautifully boned and rolled leg of lamb in the way I would cook it for myself. My table staff always passed on to me any comment or criticism of my food, should they hear any comment, flattering or critical from one of the guests. Two men were tucking into their thick slices of lamb when one of them turned to the other to say the following: "If the chef had taken this lamb out of the oven a bit sooner, we could have got this sheep back on its feet again."

I had the same problem with vegetables. I know of the amusing adage that when it comes to preparing vegetables, especially Brussels sprouts for a family Christmas: the housewife in the kitchen starts boiling them in October, ready for the big day in December. Joking apart, the majority of people do seem reluctant to eat vegetables *'al dente'* where all the flavours are retained, and they are equally reluctant to add a large knob of butter to the drained and cooked vegetables or perhaps a squeeze of lemon juice and additional pepper and salt.

An interesting episode took place at the hotel some years ago. I was in the habit of changing the menu as often as possible so that anyone staying for a week would not eat the same dish twice. I had some early arrivals just after serving breakfast, and therefore reception would offer our newly arrived guests tea and biscuits. This would give the chambermaids the opportunity to prepare the room for them as quickly as possible. After about an hour, the couple were shown to their room and shortly afterwards came to reception and said they had an unusual request. I was called to reception from my kitchen to speak to the couple because they specifically asked for the chef. A specific request? Could it be that their room at the front of the hotel overlooks a busy road with traffic lights and, despite double-glazing, is somewhat noisy? Will they want to change their room for one at the back of the hotel? Yes, there was a lift to take them to their room on the second floor, and there was plenty of space in the car park for their hire car. I just wondered what the man wanted.

He said he wanted to talk to me about food and what he can eat. I immediately passed him a copy of our weekly menu to show him exactly what to expect during his stay. He said, "I'll give this menu to my wife because she eats everything, but I only eat one thing and one thing only, and that is just chips."

"Just chips?" I responded, "what about vegetables?"

"Well, chips are vegetables, aren't they?" he replied.

"Yes, they certainly are," I replied, "well, for a change could I serve you roast or mashed potato?"

"But they are not chips," he said.

"That's true, but they are part and parcel of the same vegetable family," I suggested.

I got the message: his wife eats everything, but for the next fortnight, the husband will just eat chips. No meat or fish— just chips.

As I always had my deep-fryer ready for cooking sausages for the conventional English breakfast, I thought I should ask him what I could give him for breakfast. No prizes for guessing. He said he wanted chips. The other guests looked on in astonishment as I served him chips for breakfast. The only other problem that ensued is that other chip-loving guests wanted some of the action, and so a typical cooked breakfast turned into a mixed grill for those wishing to emulate our chip-loving aficionado.

The day that roast pork was on the menu was a favourite moment not only with the guests but above all with me, the chef. For a full house, I would take delivery of three large legs of pork and, as an extra treat, either several loins of pork or pork belly. Should there be a surplus of meat, then that would be used later in the evening for sandwiches in the bar. To obtain the finest crackling, I have always used the Chinese method of preparation. First of all, I would pour boiling hot water over the fat side of the uncooked joints, dry them completely and allow them to dry in the fridge for three hours. After that, I would make deep incisions with a very sharp knife across the dried, fat side of the joint and then rub in with my hand a generous amount of vegetable oil. I would then firmly pack the surface with sea salt and roast it in a hot oven. For the last half hour of cooking, I would baste the joints with the pan juices and, if necessary, add more salt. Once cooked and cooled, I would then put the joints in the fridge to rest. In this way, the joints would be firm enough to put through my industrial slicer so that each person would receive two thick slices along with the roast vegetables and gravy.

What I did not anticipate was what happened next. The sequel to this story involves the latest addition to our family—a beautiful boxer dog called Henry. One morning after service, I heard my sons laughing in the kitchen along with one of the waitresses. Apparently, Henry had discovered a method of opening the fridge door by bashing his snout twice against it, and then it would open with ease. Fortunately, the boys, despite enjoying what they saw, stopped

Henry from helping himself to the contents of my fridge. I never thought any more about it.

The particular day I refer to was a pork day. I was always very proud of my preparatory work regarding my favourite meat. That day I came on duty around four in the afternoon. I could not believe my eyes. What had been in the fridge, a hundred and forty slices for the guests and staff, were now reduced to about forty and of these most were strewn across the floor. The fridge door was wide open, and Henry was not visible anywhere. My assistant in the kitchen, Derek, said he knew the manager of the cold meat department at the nearby supermarket. I phoned and asked him if he could supply me with a hundred and fifty slices of pork, which, thank God, he did. Thankfully all the vegetables were intact, as were the pork stuffing and the gravy, so all I had to do was to layer the pork on a roasting dish, adding a little melted butter and just before service pop it under the grill. No complaints from the guests but it was some time before Henry could endear himself to me.

In the dining room, we always kept our wine glasses on a sideboard to make it easier for Mark or Peter to serve the guests more quickly with their drinks. However, one day a lady came to reception to say that she was a police inspector from Lancashire. She said that she did not want to get involved as she was on holiday. She went on to say that as she was coming out of the dining room, she saw two Frenchwomen take two glasses each from the sideboard and tuck them away under their bulky jackets. I thanked her for this information. Sometime later, the two French ladies came to reception to settle their bill and asked politely if there was a safe place to leave their luggage as they were leaving for St Malo on the late evening boat and had some last-minute shopping to do. They would be back in a couple of hours, they said. I carried their bags to a little room near the TV lounge and asked Sandra to keep an eye out, should the ladies return unexpectedly. With delight I went back to the little room, unzipped both bags and found my four wine glasses along with two bedroom towels which were wrapped around the stolen goods. I thought amusingly to myself that on the ferry to France they only serve wine in plastic cups, so I could just imagine these two ladies searching for the stolen glasses in which to pour their wine and then discovering that their little stolen booty had also been stolen from their bags!

*   *   *   *

When I started my business, bookings were strictly from Saturday to Saturday, but nowadays, it is totally different. One, two, and three-day stays are now the norm. When new guests arrived on a typical Saturday, fortunately, there was already a great number of regular guests who had been staying with us over the years and this mixture of newcomers and regulars made the atmosphere in the bar more amenable and relaxed. We also had a few local friends who would come in for a late drink after the nearest pub closed at eleven o'clock, and this added to the already relaxed atmosphere and made the latest arrivals truly feel at ease and welcome. The bar staff, Mark and Peter, and I had a routine to try to involve the new arrivals in the sometimes chaotic behaviour and humour that some of the locals indulged in. The following was typical of this brand of humour. The barman would say to one of the regular customers something like:

"Last night, I went out with a girl from the West Indies."

"Jamaica?"

"No, she was quite willing."

"Then I met this girl from Middlesex."

"Feltham?"

"No, but I had a good try."

"Then I met a girl from Wales."

"Bangor?"

"As a matter of fact, I did."

"Last night I went out with a girl from Ireland."

"Oh really!"

"No, O'Riley."

By this time, the new arrivals were laughing and one of them joined in with, "I met this gay guy from China…"

"Wan King!"

But this time the laughter drowned out the punch line as the bar became more relaxed and the atmosphere was good. The new guest joined in –

"I've got a gay friend in Australia."

"Sydney?"

"Oh duckie, you've been there too!"

Then we had the jokes about swingers! Songs for swinging plumbers, "Shanks for the memory".

Songs for swinging soldiers, "Tanks for the memory".

Songs for swinging bakers, "The more I knead you".

Songs for swinging Beatle fans, "The fool on the pill".

*   *   *   *

At times it was difficult to close the bar, and very often we were obliged to serve drinks until around two in the morning. Even though I had to be up early the next day to cook breakfast, I still rarely went to bed before two o'clock. Somehow there always seemed to be a man, a little bit tipsy, who just wanted to tell just about anyone who was prepared to listen about his broken marriage or a lost and abandoned relationship. It is amazing the number of personal details that come out once a person has had a good drink and the next day when you mention it, they would say, "How did you know that?"

Just next to reception is a small, narrow staircase unlike the other three which some people prefer to use, should they not wish to go up in the lift. It only has around ten steps, so anyone staying on the first floor would find it easier to access their room by using it. However, I was in reception awaiting the arrival of a group from the Midlands and talking to a French couple. Then a lady, who had previously checked in with her son was enquiring about an Island Tour booking. The son was not present, and I passed her the two tickets. Suddenly I heard someone falling down the narrow staircase. The son had made a sudden appearance. The mother did not bat an eyelid on seeing her son with his nose poised against the fitted carpet. I was naturally concerned that he may have broken a few bones and asked the mother if he was all right.

"Don't worry, pet, he never walks down the stairs at home. He just likes falling down the stairs and says it's quicker than using the stairs in the usual way." I was personally concerned, not so much for his safety because he knew the risk and enjoyed it, but I was worried in case a guest happened to be at the foot of the stairs with the intention of going up at the same time as the boy's body was in full flight coming down. Anyway, he picked himself up and went to sit in reception while his mother carried on talking as if nothing had happened. She must have heeded my warning because it never happened again.

Saturday was always the big changeover day and fortunately we had some wonderful chambermaids who, in the main, came from the island of Madeira and who worked well alongside equally hard-working girls from the UK.

I was in the kitchen cutting the chickens in half so that each guest received a leg and a breast for their dinner, along with vegetables and trimmings, when Maria rushed into the kitchen and accidentally slipped on the tiled floor that Antonio, the kitchen porter, had just mopped. She managed to get up and support herself without injury, shouting, *"Meu Deus está faltando uma janela!"* I did understand her, but then she said it in English, "No window in room 23!"

"Maria, what are you talking about? Of course, there is a window in 23! There always has been."

"It's on the bed!" she exclaimed.

I took the lift to get to the second floor and entered the room with the alleged missing window. Sometimes with foreign staff, language difficulties can arise, and comprehension of idiomatic phrases is at times lost on me when dealing with accents. But lo and behold I entered room 23, and as Maria had said correctly, the window was neatly placed across one of the two beds. I was shocked especially as the incoming guests were sitting in reception having tea and biscuits, so it was of the utmost importance that this room should be turned around as soon as possible. I went down to reception to find out who the previous occupants of this room were, fearing that they may have departed, leaving me with the expense of calling out a local company, especially at the weekend. However, I recognised the two Norwegian men who had just come through the front door and who went to put their last-minute purchases into one of the two bags left in reception. Cigarettes and booze were the two luxuries that Norwegians bought a lot of, as in their country, such purchases were extremely expensive.

"Good morning Mr Anderson; how are you?" one of the men asked me with a lispy and heavy Norwegian accent.

"Not too good," I replied. I went on, "It seems that the window in the room you both occupied is now lying across one of the beds."

"Yes," he replied, "we are not used to this heat and could not sleep, so we took it out."

"Well, Mr Engerbretsen, before you leave, I would suggest that you both go up to your former room and put it back before your taxi comes."

Neither my son Philip nor I had the technical skill necessary to do such a mammoth task. A few minutes later, I followed the men into room number 23 with a metal box full of tools to help them, but somehow they managed in next to no time to reinstall the window back on to the two brackets and hinges on which it was originally fixed. Job done, but it was a close call.

We were having a few problems with the lift. With the average age group increasing amongst our clientele, it was an essential and additional attribute to the smooth functioning of the hotel as the stairs could be a problem for those guests of a certain age whose rooms were on the second and third floor. One evening, there were sixty-five guests in the dining room, and as I was busy over the stove in my kitchen, I was unaware that two ladies had left earlier than usual. Somebody on a bed and breakfast only basis rushed to reception to inform us that screams could be heard coming from the lift shaft area. I rushed upstairs and suddenly heard muffled screams. I discovered that the lift was stuck between the first and second floor and the only way I could make contact with the two ladies was to lie down on my stomach as flat as I could and speak to them through a visible six-inch gap, and assuring them that the emergency lift service company would get them out in next to no time. I said the most stupid thing: "Keep calm and stay where you are," to which one of the ladies replied, "We're not bloody well going anywhere, we're stuck—just get us out!" Then I remembered an old post-war film with, I think John Mills, when singing to people in danger was the thing to do to bolster their morale. Unfortunately, I chose to hum a Beatle song, 'We All Live in a Yellow Submarine', which was a bad choice. A young guest walking down the corridor giggled and said a song by the Animals would be more appropriate and started humming 'We Gotta Get Out of This Place'. I kept on apologising to the trapped ladies and after about half an hour, the lift mechanics arrived and managed to raise the lift-cage to the second floor. I was there to greet them and expressed my sincere regret at their being trapped. I took up a tray of tea and biscuits to their room. I learned the reason why they had both left the dining room prematurely. They had both taken laxatives and desperately needed to use the toilet.

A man and his wife checked in for a week and immediately asked for the bar. Reception informed them that it did not open until six in the evening, but in the meantime, they could have a glass of whatever they required although it would be served in the reception or the TV lounge.

"No, we want a proper drink," he replied.

"Well, aren't two drinks a good starter?" reception asked.

"No," he went on, "we are big wine drinkers, so we will need five bottles of your house red wine to get us through the day." So reception gave them five bottles, two glasses and a bottle opener. In all the years of running the hotel, I have never seen two people consume so much wine. This was a daily routine, so by the end of the week, they had consumed thirty-five bottles of house red! In addition to this marathon drinking, they also popped into the bar for the occasional glass of red wine. Strangely enough, their behaviour was impeccable, and they never showed any signs of being inebriated.

By contrast, we had another couple who also stayed for a week and from our wine list chose a bottle of wine called Black Tower, a wine in a similar category but not quite as agreeable as Liebfraumilch. I think they chose Black Tower because it was easier to pronounce than the other labels which were mostly shown in French. Every evening the waitress would put the bottle in the fridge to keep for the following day, but it seemed that they must each have consumed just a thimbleful of this wine each day, as on the last day of their stay, there were still two generous shots left in the bottle. I had totally forgotten about this bottle, as I was busy with a special request from a French guest who wanted chicken chasseur instead of the fixed menu, so I cooked the chicken with shallots, mushrooms and shouted to Antonio to pass me some special white wine that I kept in a box. He poured the wine into a jug and gave it to me. Without thinking, I poured the wine into the frying pan to finish the dish and allowed it to reduce for five minutes. When the couple asked for their bottle of Black Tower, I realised what had happened. I had used their wine in my chicken dish, so I asked Mark, the barman, to get a similar bottle from the bin, wash it out thoroughly and put in anything that looked similar to what they had all week. No, they did not notice any difference, and the Frenchman was complimentary about my chicken chasseur—not aware that it contained a German wine—sacrilege to a Frenchman!

*   *   *   *

A barman who worked in another St Helier hotel often came in for a drink, and we used to exchange funny anecdotes regarding the unusual behavioural patterns of some of our guests. "I had a funny one last night..." he started.

Before I continue with this story, I must explain that we have a castle out at sea, yet just a few hundred metres from the promenade called Elizabeth Castle, where Sir Walter Raleigh resided as the Governor of Jersey in the year 1600. When the tide is out, you can walk there in about twenty minutes. When the tide is in, a small boat service is available to take the visitor there in just a few minutes.

The barman continued, "So I asked our two guests if they had a nice day, and if so, what did they do?"

"We had a lovely day; in fact, we went to Guernsey," replied the husband, "it's a very small island. In fact, it took us no time to walk around it."

"Did you go by boat or plane?" he asked.

"No," replied the wife, "I can't stand flying, so we walked there; it only took us about half an hour, what with my husband's bad leg."

"I think you are mistaken," continued the barman, "because Guernsey is not part of Jersey, and in fact, you walked to Elizabeth Castle, and that *is* in Jersey."

A good majority of our bookings are from regular guests and recommendations, but nowadays the internet plays an important role in boosting our numbers, especially from contacts such as Booking.com. I have always endeavoured to discover how people found out about us, so one evening, I noticed that there was a man on his own in the bar drinking a pint of lager. I went over to introduce myself and informed him that I would like to know how he found the hotel because I knew that the booking did not come through an agency or the net.

In a very strong and melodic Welsh accent, he went on to explain, "Well, as is my habit, I went to the Working Man's Club in Cardiff, where I am a member and went to the bar to have my pint. All I heard from a man standing at the bar talking to another customer were the following words: 'That was the finest steak and kidney pie I have ever eaten in my life'. So, I went over to the man in question and asked where I could find this pie, and he gave me your address. That's why I'm here."

Talking to other hoteliers, it is remarkable how many have, like us, their own individual and unusual stories to tell concerning their guests. One nearby hotel had a very amusing manager named Joe, who was invariably on top form, ready to tell a joke whether with his guests or with his staff. He was normally the most cheerful of men and would pop into our bar just for half an hour to get away from his own guests, but that particular evening, he came in with a long face, looking very depressed. I poured a brandy which was unusual for him, as he always drank gin and tonic. I asked him why he looked so sad.

"Well," he started, "I have just been to a funeral involving just three people. There was the man in the coffin, his wife and just me. I didn't even know the man!" He went on, "Well, this couple checked into the hotel with their daughter, and after a few days, the man had a heart attack during the night and unfortunately died in his room. It was my responsibility as manager to console the wife and delicately break the sad news to his daughter, who was in a single room nearby. She came to the door looking a little dishevelled and rubbing her eyes. As sensitively as I could, I told her that her father had unfortunately passed away with a heart attack."

"Oh, Jesus Christ, trust him to bloody well ruin our holiday—was he pissed?" she replied. She closed the door in Joe's face and went back to bed. He never saw her again until the day of her departure. She didn't even turn up at the funeral. That is why Joe represented the hotel and gave the man's wife some moral support.

Just then, another barman, Eamonn, who worked with Joe, came in for his usual drink before going to work. He could not speak a word of French, but whenever he popped in, he would always do an absolutely perfect impersonation of someone speaking the language, and I would reply to his nonsensical dissertation in correct French. The English guests would be impressed with his performance which sounded a little bit like Peter Sellers' Inspector Clouseau in *The Pink Panther*. Anyway, he left the bar and went to start his night shift. For a moment, I forgot about the French couple from Rennes who were sitting in the corner, he with a Pastis, she with a Kir Royale. The man came up to the bar and in French said, "I didn't really understand what that man was saying, but I know he was speaking some sort of French. I just wondered which part of France did he come from."

That's how convincing Eamonn's French was!

We had a booking for a party of fifty-four guests from an address in Surrey. Sometimes I used to try to guess the type of person who could be our prospective guest. When the two coaches arrived at the front door, I could see that every person, except for two, were black. They were all so jovial and what I noticed was the way they were dressed. Every man, with very few exceptions, wore a suit with a very colourful shirt, matching tie and shiny shoes. The women were also very well turned out. I was told that they all belonged to the same social club, and this was their annual outing. I must add that over the years, I have rarely seen so many people looking so spotlessly clean from a personal and clothing point of view. There were no problems with food. They seemed to enjoy everything I put before them. Many were originally from Jamaica, so for them, I tried to spice up some of the typical English food that I would normally serve by adding chilli, red peppers and serving something that resembled jerk pork. They were very grateful for my effort.

The next day a local shopkeeper came up to me as I was emptying the dustbin and asked me if all the black people were staying in my hotel. I said that they were and that they were such charming people.

"Well," replied the shopkeeper, "when I saw them all together walking down the road, I thought it was an oil slick!" suddenly bursting into raucous laughter.

I gave him one of my disapproving looks and said, "I bet you wouldn't say that to their face if they came into your shop and spent a lot on purchases!" I think he got the message.

$$* \qquad * \qquad * \qquad *$$

I am sure that every hotelier has similar stories to tell, but the following incident happened one Sunday morning during the busiest time of the year. Every Sunday, I would reverse the usual routine by offering our guests lunch instead of the evening meal. The guests seemed to prefer this arrangement, and it suited us as the staff could then have the rest of the day off after serving lunch. Just before service, I always visited my brother Derek's hotel, the Grange

Court, which was situated a few minutes away from my hotel. He and I would have a quick drink together and discuss trends in the season and how our respective businesses were progressing. It was very quiet in his hotel with not a single person anywhere—just staff doing the necessary little jobs before serving lunch.

"But Derek, where is everybody? Your bar is empty," I said.

"Well," he replied, "believe it or not, we've got a full house; in fact, sixty people, but they have just been picked up by two coaches to take them on an island tour before they have lunch. That's why it is dead quiet."

Suddenly the fire alarms started blaring out. Derek and I looked at each other, both knowing that this can happen without necessarily having a fire, so we did not panic. However, we went into the hallway to investigate and looked up the stairs from where this infernal noise emanated. Never in our lives had we ever experienced what happened next. A massive plume of smoke was coming from somewhere on the first floor, and on every level, the noise of the fire alarms multiplied. Derek rushed into the kitchen and phoned the emergency services for assistance. In the meantime, the fire had spread across the whole of the first floor and progressed to the bar where, minutes before, Derek and I were having a drink together. I quickly wedged the door to stop the fire from spreading and what I saw next was quite remarkable. The flames had now arrived in the bar ceiling just above the spirit optics, which were on the top shelf. Suddenly, there were multiple explosions with corks exiting from spirit bottles making a popping noise and bottles cascading down on to the floor.

The fire brigade arrived while I was at the bottom of the stairs to direct the firemen to where the flames were coming from, but to them, it was obvious. One fireman must have thought I was the chef in Derek's hotel as I was dressed like one in my kitchen gear. I thought I was being helpful, but one fireman told me in no uncertain terms to get out of his way. I cannot repeat his language, but he was

116

just doing his job and doing it efficiently. I believe what he said rhymed with 'clucking bell' and worse. Soon the fire spread rapidly, and suddenly, there was a whole team of additional firemen. Within minutes the fire was under control. The smell left behind, the odour of burnt furniture, scorched walls, in fact, everything in the path of the fire could be smelt throughout the building.

When all the guests returned from their coach trip, there was shock and panic because not only would the hotel have to close immediately, but the guests would have to be found alternative accommodation. They also had to go up the wringing wet stairs to see what they could salvage from the chaos. By the end of the day, we helped to accommodate all the guests in various hotels around the island. That was not easy as it was the peak season. We could only thank our lucky stars that the fire did not happen during the night because, without doubt, that would have caused multiple deaths. The fire brigade carried out an investigation as to the cause of the fire, but nothing concrete was deduced from the enquiry. I personally feel it could have been a faulty television because that was one of the very first objects the fire crew threw down the stairs, smouldering as it reached the ground floor. Full credit to all the emergency services—they were magnificent.

My Big Mistake in the Kitchen

In later years, most of the staff we employed were Portuguese and I must say that without their dedicated assistance and hard work in Jersey, we would be a lot poorer culturally and socially without their sterling qualities. Unfortunately, language, especially English, was at times a problem; getting the waitress to pronounce items from the sweet trolley was sometimes a linguistic minefield. A simple sentence such as, "Madam, would you like some trifle?" became slightly distorted into, "Hey laid(lady!) you want tripe (trifle)?"

It was a particularly busy night in the bar. It had been a wonderful day weather-wise with plenty of sunshine and everyone seemed to have changed colour in just a few hours. The hotel was full and all the guests seemed to be in the bar drinking and singing along to Stevie Wonder on the juke-box. It is only when someone fails to put money in the jukebox that you can actually hear what people are saying. It was one of those moments I can recall when two young men at the bar were discussing the fate of a friend who had committed some misdemeanour in the UK and who was now on probation. They did not say what crime had been carried out but listening to them I heard the word "break-in" so I assumed it was a question of some form of robbery. They realised that I was aware of their conversation and humbly asked my advice. I simply replied that I hoped their mutual friend would see the error of his ways and honourably accept his punishment and perhaps turn over a new leaf.

"Have you never been tempted to break the law?" asked the younger of the two men.

I then went on in a somewhat juvenile and immature way and explained that when I started with only six rooms, saving money was of the utmost importance. I said that I had an arrangement with a local farmer to deliver two sacks of potatoes every week and that I would pay him by cheque on the dot every month. Then one day the usual delivery driver arrived with my usual two sacks of potatoes and whispered "Quick, only 15 shillings a bag, cash please" and put them on the steps of my kitchen.

I replied "No, I have an account with your boss and I pay monthly"

He looked shocked and said "You missed the point guvnor, you won't get a better price than that anywhere" he growled.

"Are you telling me that these spuds fell off the back of a lorry?" I replied.

"Well, well……" he mumbled.

I said "Don't you ever offer me stolen goods again because if you do I will denounce you to your employer".

I did not tell his boss about his thieving but informed him that I did not want that particular employee near my premises again. I simply made the excuse that he was extremely rude to me. I never saw him again.

I think my feeble story seemed somewhat bizarre and simplistic to the two young men and not worthy of even discussing for a second. Compared to the fate of their mutual friend on bail, my story seemed trivial.

"But that was cheap for a bag of spuds, I would have bought them even though they were stolen" said the younger one.

"It certainly was cheap but once you go down that slippery slope..." I did not finish my sentence because I had to serve a customer. During my conversation with the two young men I noticed a man of about fifty years of age listening intently to what I was saying. I shall call him Mr X.

He said, "It depends if you get caught, but sometimes it's worth the risk."

I then told him a genuine story of how guilt feels in the most petty and insignificant way. I was driving for the very first time in Spain with my family, just past Valencia when I took a secondary road and found myself on a deserted track of a minor road, but on either side there were orange trees in full blossom. Without thinking I went over and picked just two oranges, peeled them and shared them with my family. Nobody was around to see me do this, but I still regarded this as stealing.

Mr X said "I did something once but I did it with a great deal of thought".

He went on "You cannot condemn those two lads for their views, their mate was just unlucky and got caught. Listen I want to tell you just how the system works. I've got a small family-run garage and like all businesses we go through some very challenging moments when we cannot pay our bills. I wasn't selling many cars and petrol sales were in those days on ration, so I had to do something to solve the financial problem. So, I sent my boy around to the garage late one night with half a gallon of petrol and a box of matches and he set fire to it which completely incinerated the premises, but solved the money problem".

By this time the jukebox was silent and I told Mr X that amongst the holidaymakers there could be policemen present and advised him to be careful as to what he would say next. His voice was loud. He simply said, "Well the Insurance Company paid up to the tune of £25,000... problem solved! so here I am in Jersey celebrating."

Mark was a very efficient barman from Glasgow who had a good sense of humour and was a fervent supporter of Celtic Football Club. Just to tease him I pretended to support fierce rivals Glasgow Rangers. He would jokingly refer to me as a "currant bun", slang for a Hun or Proddy, slang for a protestant. I did not take offence as neither terminology was applicable to me. I did not do the following to antagonise him but this is what happened. All my life I have been against gambling. Business being at times a massive challenge made me respect the money earned through hard work. So, one evening my son Alan, who then worked in a Betting shop popped in for a drink and we started talking about the World Cup. This was 1990. Alan said that Scotland would demolish Costa Rica, which brought a smile to Mark's face. I asked Alan about the chances of Costa Rica beating Scotland, to which he replied, "No chance, Dad that will never happen".

I went on to say that sometimes the underdog comes out on top. I then asked Alan the odds for Costa Rica to win.

"Dad you have always told me not to gamble. Now I'm telling you that it is 10-1 for a Costa Rica win, so don't waste your money-just have a drink!"

I went to my office and counted out £100. I then gave this to my son to put on a Costa Rica win. I thought this is my first ever bet so maybe I'll have beginner's luck.

To everybody's surprise Costa Rica won 1-0. I received a thousand pounds the following day and Mark did not take this news too well. He enquired how I could bet against his country and at the same time make money from his country's loss. It took some time before normal relations between us were restored.

"Mark, I did not do it to offend you" I told him.

"But you made £1,000 betting on Scotland to lose" he replied

"Thank God the National team contained a mixture of Proddy/Huns and Roman Candles" I replied somewhat sarcastically but I think diplomatically.

My daughter-in-law Christine took charge of the hotel's early-morning breakfast, catering for seventy guests. This needed a great deal of organisation and meant an early start at around 6 o'clock every morning. But this particular day would turn out to be a most unusual one that she will certainly never forget. One of her first routines was to check the automatic switch on the front door and disable it so that guests could come and go as they please. As she approached the front door, she not only realised that someone had forgotten to close it but observed the arrival of a most unusual guest. It was neither man, woman nor child. The arrival turned out to be a most beautiful Jersey calf that must have fallen off the back of a lorry on its way to the abattoir. It was poised just a few inches from the entrance, so Christine picked it up and put it into the small garden area at the side of the hotel. Then she gave it water to drink and some cereals in a bowl. Despite plenty of publicity from the local media nobody came forward to claim it, so it was suggested that it should be taken to a sanctuary somewhere in the north of the island. We went to visit the calf whose name "Mornington" is inscribed on a nameplate along with the history as to how it got there after its brief encounter at the hotel reception. When the guests discovered what had happened, they all went into the garden and took photographs of the very young children who were stroking and caressing it. They were in their element to see such a most unusual and unexpected visitor, who had somehow avoided the traffic in one of Jersey's busiest thoroughfares only to make its way to safety and a new life in another part of the island. Needless to say that one of the guests with a sharp sense of humour said to the other guests who were admiring and stroking the new arrival "It was on its way to be slaughtered, but may it now live happily "heifer" after.

Looking back over the years, I have to cringe at some of the mistakes I inadvertently and innocently made. This is confession time, and I think, my worst mistake ever. A young guest arrived, and I noticed that he was wearing a skull cap or kippah, so to make him feel more at ease, I welcomed him with the Hebrew term 'shalom'. He asked me how I knew this word, meaning peace, and I explained that I had visited Israel, which pleased him. He told me that he was training to be a rabbi and had to follow a very strict code of religious practice, and that affected all aspects of everyday life, including the food he consumed. I said I would carry out his wishes to respect his code of religious practice. Later that morning, he returned with a beautiful piece of sirloin steak to be prepared according to his wishes. I told him that I always had sirloin steak available in my fridge and that he did not need to buy it, but he insisted on buying his own. He said that the steak had to be heavily covered with sea salt on both sides to draw out any excess blood over several hours. I completely obeyed his wishes and packed the steak with sea salt very firmly and covered it with clingfilm. It had to stay in the fridge for the next seven hours. After this time, I took it out, brushed off the salt and dried it with kitchen paper, so no blood was visible. It was now ready for use when required. I informed the Portuguese waitress that it was important for the guest to tell me exactly when he was ready to eat his steak. It was a very busy Saturday, one I'll never forget. There were arrivals from early morning till the evening. We operate a fixed but flexible menu, and this particular evening there were several people, mostly French, who asked for steak and not chicken. I was so busy with the chicken orders that I shouted at Antonio to fetch me a steak from the fridge. He passed me a nice sirloin and as usual, I would give my skillet pan loads of heat and after four minutes, drop in just a very small hint of pork fat (a trick I learnt in France). Once the meat was sealed, then I added a knob of butter, seasoned the steak with salt and black pepper and cooked it for four minutes either side. Job done—or so I thought. In passing, I told the waitress that she must look after the man with the skull cap and to let me know when he has finished his first course. There was silence. I knew something was wrong. She blushed and told me that the steak I had just cooked was not for the French man who did not like chicken, but she had given it to the man with the skull cap. I felt embarrassed and angry. The evening did not go well for me. I had this problem on my mind and later that evening, when I was about to go into the bar, I saw the young trainee rabbi coming towards me.

"I just want to say something," he started.

Whoops, I thought, *confession time, here goes my reputation.*

"I just want to say that the sirloin steak was just about the best I have ever eaten; what's the secret?" he continued.

"No secret," I replied, "just happy that you enjoyed it!"

*   *   *   *

With the hotel well and truly established, Sandra and I agreed that we could now manage on the summer income without being obliged to open in the winter. Now that the family was growing up, we decided to take the boys away on a proper holiday instead of returning to and staying with our respective families in England. I had spoken to my neighbour Roy about our forthcoming holiday, and he said that he had been to somewhere that, at the time, I had never heard of. He described it as a small and typical Spanish fishing village called Benidorm. This resort is now known to everybody because of its dubious reputation, but at the time, it really was a simple retreat, ideal for family holidays. We took the boat to St Malo in my brand new, blue Renault 16. Jersey now operates a drive-on car ferry service, but in those days, a big crane would hoist the car on to the boat in St Helier Harbour, and the French would unload the vehicles on to the quayside in St Malo, assuming the French dockers were not on strike, which always seemed to be the case whenever we used that service. Because of the striking dockers, we invariably had to spend the first night in a charming little family hotel called La Noguette, which is to this day still there but trading under a different name.

The next day we all scrambled into the car, and I drove through Brittany using only secondary roads, which for the boys was a good and authentic way of seeing the real France. We drove through the town of Rennes, then passed through Clisson, and it was at that moment that I started to think about where we should stay for the night. That place would be Brive, where I spent such a happy few weeks at the age of fourteen with my French family. We arrived there late afternoon, and I did to the family exactly what I have done ever since. I gathered them all on the steps of the church opposite 'Opticien Mazet' and made them look up at the little first-floor window that constituted my bedroom above the optician's shop. I can never go to that region of France without standing on the church steps and carrying out this ritual. For my long-suffering family, it was a routine they found quite boring.

Two days later, we arrived in Benidorm after having spent a night in a large family room in a simple but clean *pensión* near Zaragoza. It was the month of October when we arrived and unlike the tourist town it is today, at that time of year it was very quiet. The weather was warm, and we would watch the fishermen organising their nets for their next trip out to sea. I managed to find a ground-floor flat to rent at a very reasonable price with a parking space for the Renault. We were all extremely happy, and as a treat, we would visit some of the local restaurants—one in particular. Maybe time plays havoc with one's memory, but this place served the most delicious 'steak a la pimienta'—this time it was not served with the classic *flambé* with brandy and cream but with a dark *'bouillon'* reduction. For me, just being away from my stove made this meal extra special and memorable.

It was good to be away from Jersey and the hotel, but time seemed to pass very quickly—two weeks just disappeared, but we loved every moment. However, driving back through Spain and then France was like having another holiday. So, on the last night in Benidorm, I thought I would spoil the family with one last meal. It was not our usual 'peppered steak' restaurant but a hotel along the beach. To get to the restaurant on the second floor, we had to take the lift. We all crammed in as best as we could. One sweet, little lady joined us just before the door closed. She was friendly and started patting Jonathan on the head.

"And where are you from?" she asked in a strong Glaswegian accent.

"Jersey, Madam," I replied.

"Oh," she continued, "I've got a close friend who goes to Jersey every year, and she wouldn't go anywhere else but Jersey. Tell me, have you heard of the Mornington Hotel?"

I was cautious because ever sensitive of criticism but loving praise, I said, "Yes, it is a town hotel in St Helier."

"Well, my friend says it is the best hotel she has ever stayed in, and as for the food, well, that also is the best."

I then shocked her by saying that we were the owners. She was quite taken aback by what I said and delighted that she could return to Scotland and tell her friend that she had met the owners of her favourite hotel. As we got out of the lift, she stroked Jonathan's cheek and planted a small kiss on his forehead.

As this would be our last meal in Benidorm, I wanted the boys and Sandra to be a little more adventuresome with their choice of food, instead of constantly playing safe with dishes that they felt more at home with, so I ordered *'calamares fritos'*, the famous squid deep fried in rings and served with a dip-in sauce. They loved it—it just made a change from egg and chips.

The next day we left Benidorm and made our way towards the Spanish border town of Jonquera. Just before the border, we had to stop the car because Jonathan would not do what every self-respecting Spanish or French boy would do naturally, and that is to pee against the nearest tree. So, we all went into a café so that he could use a conventional toilet. I ordered coffee for Sandra and myself, and the boys asked for Coca-Cola. I heard two attractive girls speaking English together with a strong Cockney accent. One of them must have seen the GBJ sticker on the car and, with a real East End accent, said, "Oi mate, what's wiv the GBJ and what the bleedin' 'ell does that stands for?"

I replied, "Have a guess."

"I ain't got the foggiest idea," she shouted, "the only place I can fink of with a 'J' is Jerusalem."

"I said, "It stands for 'Great Britain Jersey'."

"Never 'eard of it," she replied.

A waiter suddenly appeared to clear the glasses off the table of the Cockney girls and spoke to the girls in Spanish. I thought there was no point in doing that because they'll never understand him as they could hardly speak English. Suddenly she said, "*¿Puede indicarme donde están los servicios?*" I was so impressed that I asked her to write it down for me. Like Jonathan, she was asking for the toilet. She said that she and her girl friend had been working in a bar in Lloret del Mar as waitresses, mainly serving English holidaymakers but also going out with a few local boys, and that is how they both had a working knowledge of the language. In fact, thanks to this chance meeting, I was influenced and encouraged to start learning Spanish on my return to Jersey.

"See ya, mate, 'ave a good journey!" she shouted as we left the café and made our way back to the car. Our plan was to leave Spain in the next hour and travel through France to arrive in Normandy and beyond to take the car ferry from Calais to Dover because we decided that it would be a good idea to visit our respective parents in England.

We had to spend our last night in a small hotel near Calvados which had a very lively bar a few yards from the reception. I left the family in the car while I walked inside to check if there were two rooms available. Luckily there was just one large family room left, so I went back to the car to tell Sandra and the boys that we had a room for the night. As I walked through to the reception, I had to pass through a passageway, which on both sides was bustling with young men and women drinking, laughing and talking loudly. They all seemed to be around my age; some were younger, but as I walked through to check in, I felt all eyes were on me as I held young Jonathan's hand. Sandra and the boys followed closely behind.

I still think it was wonderful marrying at such an early age, and becoming parents to our four sons. I felt that growing up with them would make us all feel like brothers together. However, seeing all the young people drinking and hugging each other in the bar gave me the feeling of having missed out on a tiny segment of life that I had never experienced. It was the way they looked at me. Was it a look of admiration or sympathy? I tried to convince myself that it was more a look of approbation than critical sympathy, but that look stayed with me for years to come.

We reached Calais the next day and boarded the ferry for Dover. We spent a week with our families, and suddenly I realised I was missing Jersey, so I then decided to leave England and return home. The Renault 16 behaved herself, so before driving down to Southampton to board the ferry to Jersey, I thought it beneficial for the boys to see a little bit of London and in particular to show them where I was born and where I attended school along Victoria Embankment. After that we drove along Whitehall and suddenly I realised from my days at school that Downing Street was not too far away. Something that is hard to believe nowadays is what happened next. I recognised immediately the turning that would lead me into Downing Street. I indicated my intention to turn into perhaps the most famous street in the UK and a policeman very kindly stopped the oncoming traffic to allow me to do just that. My little Renault 16 may have seemed somewhat out of place in such distinguished surroundings, but there, right opposite the front door of number 10, we stayed as a family watching all the activity of people arriving and leaving, hoping to perhaps get a glimpse of the new Prime Minister, Harold Wilson, but this was not to be. We all stayed there for around twenty minutes without any problems at all. Eventually, a policeman with a soft Irish accent very politely said that if we didn't mind, he would request that we move on as other cars, carrying members of the Government were due to arrive at any moment and would need to park where we had been for twenty minutes. The idea of such a scenario happening in today's political climate amidst the violence and demonstrations that society has grown used to is unthinkable.

*   *   *   *

The memory of the Cockney girl speaking Spanish stayed with me and played on my mind, so the first thing I did on my return was to order a Linguaphone Spanish language course. I worked on it day and night, and since the hotel was closed in the winter, I decided I could do more to improve my knowledge of the language. Even after just a few weeks of repetitive sentences, I already knew that I could do better. I have always been influenced by people for whom I have had admiration, so my desire to learn Spanish was due to my encounter with the Cockney girl near Zaragoza. Even after just a few weeks, my Spanish was reasonable, but there was room for improvement.

I broke the news to Sandra two weeks later. I had made enquiries about a language school in Malaga and decided that I would enrol in a crash course at this school—*Escuela de Lenguas*

Extranjeras. I had the Renault thoroughly serviced, bade farewell to Sandra and the boys and took myself and the car to St Malo.

I spent the first night in a small, simple and reasonably-priced hotel called Hotel Surcouf. In the dining room, there was only another couple eating. For me, eating alone was a completely new experience—one that I would grow to like. In the past we went everywhere together, so for me, this was a totally new experience but a welcoming one. No more four Coca-Colas for the boys, no wine for Sandra—just me. I went to a table, and the waitress gave me the menu. I then realised I could eat whatever I wanted to. In hindsight, I consider this meal as one of the most memorable ever. With just myself to worry about, I did not have to skimp. I started with the most delicious *'Moules Marinières'* followed by a rib-eye steak, beautifully sealed with a pepper sauce and a mountain of real chips. I ordered a most unusual wine, a half bottle of the blood-red wine of Cahors. I skipped dessert but had a plate of Camembert and Roquefort cheese with crusty bread. After that feast, I ordered a *'noisette'* (small white coffee) and, for the first time in ages, a Courvoisier brandy. I was beginning to enjoy my own company, but I feared that this wonderful feeling would, in time, wear off and I would return to normality again.

On my way down, I naturally stopped in Brive and spent the night in Le Chapon Fin hotel. The next day I ordered a bouquet of flowers from the same shop, where fifteen years previously I bought flowers for Madame Mazet, who so kindly looked after me when I was fourteen years old. I walked into the shop and said, "These flowers are for you, Madame Mazet"

She said to me in French, "You have the wrong Madame Mazet, you need my daughter-in-law who is also Madame Mazet."

Well this was understandable because she had not seen me in fifteen years, and now I was taller, weighing more and had a moustache.

"Mon dieu, tu fais toujours des bêtises," she said teasing me about buying the flowers. I said a quick *"bonjour"* to all the family and the opticians working in the back of the shop. Jacques was not there. He was out on his bike again.

My Brive pilgrimage was over, but before I got into the car, I glanced back at the large area between Monsieur Mazet's shop and my hotel and remembered the evening when in 1952, France's arguably greatest singer Gilbert Bécaud sang on a raised auditorium to an audience of three thousand young people to celebrate the annual anniversary of the liberation of France from German occupation. I was fourteen years of age and immediately became a fan of this great singer with the raucous voice, known as "Monsieur 100,000 volts".

From Brive, I drove directly to the French border town of Le Perthus and then crossed into Spain and drove from La Jonquera on the Spanish side until late at night. It was about eleven o'clock and I was exhausted after the long drive. The only time I stopped was for petrol. Unlike the French, the Spanish eat a lot later, but I thought that even at this late hour, I would be lucky to find something to eat. I was driving north-east of Murcia and was getting somewhat concerned and frustrated at not finding a small hotel open. I continued driving across what seemed like barren land when suddenly I saw in the distance a flickering light next to a sign saying *'Hostal'*. I could hardly believe my eyes. I stopped the car and entered what looked like a French *'routier'* as I could see a battalion of lorries in the car park. Luckily, the lady in charge spoke French, so she was able to offer me a very small room. I was shown up to my room by a young boy with a humped back and who was sadly slightly disabled, both physically and speech-wise. I put my fingers to my mouth as if I were eating, and he understood immediately and pointed to show me where I could find something to eat. I followed the direction of his hand. Even though it was eleven-thirty at night, I was surprised that I could still be served. As I approached a wide door on the ground floor, I could hear muffled voices and shouting.

I was shocked to see a massive twenty-foot long oblong table and around it, about eighteen men. They were not eating, and the paper napkins had not been used, so I was in luck with my timing. I certainly felt the odd man out, but they were polite and welcoming. They just went on with speaking to me in Spanish. Somehow with my limited knowledge, I understood that they were on their way to deliver goods in Malaga.

There was no menu, but two waitresses just put down in front of each driver a massive bowl of chicken soup with noodles. For the main course, half a chicken with loads of chips and a green salad with a sprinkling of red and green peppers. After the dessert, I think one of the drivers must have felt sorry for me because when I was drinking my *'cortado'* (small white coffee), he sent over a large glass of Fundador brandy and raised both thumbs. In his direction, I shouted, *"Muchas gracias."*

I went straight to my room and fell asleep immediately.

*   *   *   *

I arrived in Rincón de la Victoria early in the afternoon. This was the small village recommended by the school where there was reasonably-priced accommodation. I checked into a small hotel, and apart from a retired Englishman, who was bald, rotund and well-spoken, I was the only other guest. After all, it was November. I had a very simple meal that evening, and even though the other guest was English, I kept my distance from him. He had his table; I had mine. He had the bearing of an ex-military chap, so I nicknamed him 'the Major'.

The next day I enrolled in the *Escuela de idiomas extranjeras.* Surprisingly, the principal of the school was an ex-American military serviceman who had been badly injured in Vietnam and could only walk comfortably with the aid of crutches. I was informed by another pupil that the principal, too, held the rank of major. Somehow, I felt that he took an immediate dislike to me the moment he checked me in at reception. There was only one other Englishman on the course, and his name was David Hart. I started my lessons on a one-to-one basis, and in particular, I got to know my teacher, Don José, and his wife, whose parents were Spanish, although she had been brought up and educated in England. Opposite the school was a bar very close to the beach, and David, especially after a few drinks, would tell the most outrageous but respectable jokes. He made me laugh a lot, and it was at that very moment when the American major hobbled over in my direction and said something that surprised me: "You have a very loud laugh."

"Well," I replied, "if you could hear some of David's jokes, I think even you would have a little laugh."

He answered, "English humour, I suppose."

"Yes," I replied, "the best!"

The next day at school, the American seemed more conciliatory. I was just going into class when he came up to me and asked me a favour.

"The English teacher is ill. I would like you to take his place. You will have a mixed class of thirteen Spanish and French students, and I want you to explain to them how your Parliamentary system works and then give them a lesson in affirmatives and negatives in speech."

I said I would be pleased to do that for him.

He said, "I don't suppose you have any qualification to teach, but you do realise that you would be doing me a big favour?"

He seemed to be much more congenial than he had been the day before.

"As a matter of fact, I am a Chartered Linguist at the Institute of Linguists in London but only in French and not Spanish," I replied.

He seemed slightly surprised by my response. "Give it your best—your class is in the second room on the right. They are waiting for you."

As I opened the door, I must confess that it was with a great deal of trepidation, as I had never taught English to foreign students professionally before. As I entered the classroom, half of them were about to stand up, but I gestured to them to remain seated. They all had a working knowledge of English, some a lot more than others. There was a long rectangular oak table, and around it were thirteen pairs of eyes staring at me. Seven adult males and six women, some of whom were French, which made me feel more at ease, language-wise. I introduced myself and started talking about the English Parliament and the number of seats necessary to fill the House of Commons. I remembered then that it comprised approximately around six hundred or more members. I spoke particularly slowly so that they could understand me.

After that, I continued the lesson with the study of affirmatives and negatives. While looking a moment at the students and their reaction, I noticed that at the opposite end of the table, facing me was a young man about twenty-three years of age with a compulsive and permanently fixed stare and grin on his face—not an offensive grin but somehow I sensed a little trouble brewing as he looked a little naïve, but not in a threatening way. I started my first affirmative, then negative statements by giving them the following examples.

"I eat." "I do not eat."

I made them shout these words in unison until it was word perfect. Then individually, I went to each student, and to the first one, I said, "I know," and they all shouted, "I do not know", without being prompted. I went through all the everyday words. The result was encouraging. I then tried a different verb. The young man with the staring eyes looked at me as if to say, "What about me?" I thought a little and said to him, "You can."

He replied, "You do not can."

"No, no," I replied, "we'll try a different route. Try this one "you will" becomes "you won't" so can you try again with "you can?""

The guy with the eyes shouted, "You c...!" He thought he did well and shouted it out twice again. The rest were about to join in with him.

I was firm with them and said it is an offensive word and must never, ever be used again. I shouted, "'You can' becomes 'you cannot'."

They repeated it to perfection. An embarrassing moment resolved, but one of the French women students still did not understand why I was so vehement in condemning this grotesque and impolite word and asked me what it meant. I told her the French equivalent was *'foufoune'*. She looked embarrassed and didn't say another word.

The bell rang, so I got up to leave, but the class wanted more. They asked me where I was going. I said I was going across to the beach bar to have a drink. They asked if they could join me and continue the lesson over lunch and a few glasses of wine. I was truly flattered by this compliment and said I would willingly love to impart my knowledge of the English language to them. As I went ahead of them, the man with the starry eyes tugged at my sleeve and said to me very slowly, "You cannot," which he repeated three times... "and not c..." he added with a twinkle in his eye. That is something neither of us will ever forget.

Apart from having a regular drink with the only English student, David, I had a policy of only mixing socially with Spanish people, as I knew that if I wanted to speak fluent Spanish, that was the only way to go. I visited several Spanish homes, and after a month, I felt that I had made enormous progress. Looking back, it was, I think, that chance meeting near Zaragoza with the two Cockney girls that encouraged me to learn this beautiful language.

The month passed quickly. Obviously, I kept in contact with my family in Jersey, but suddenly, I felt this need to reinvent myself. I was unaccustomed to this degree of freedom. I left Rincón de la Victoria and, on the way home, stopped off in L' Orient, because one of the French lady students in my class had invited me to have dinner with her family and stay in a nearby hotel. After a superb meal and a comfortable night's stay I drove directly to St Malo and fortunately the French dockers were not on strike that weekend, so there was no delay in arriving back home in Jersey.

Looking around the hotel, I realised that there was a lot of painting and decorating to do ready for the summer season. So, after a few days of getting back to family life, I started my work in earnest and began by painting corridors and bedrooms one after the other. I know that the little spell in Spain unsettled me somewhat. It was a freedom that I was totally unaccustomed to, and I found that I was missing the casual and temporary joys of being alone. However, the business is and always will be a priority because I realised that without it, we could not do the things that we had now become accustomed to, especially as the boys were getting older and needed further education.

Sandra and I separated a year later. It was so sad because she was a good mother and at the same time such a formidable and hard-working person. Her loyal contribution to the running of the business was one of the many reasons why, to this day, it is a success. The boys handled the new domestic arrangement with dignity and realism.

It was strange at first being alone but slowly and surely, I got used to the new situation, and I began to enjoy it. I also had the support of excellent staff who helped me in the most understanding way. John and his wife Pauline were of the utmost importance to the continued success of the hotel and contributed to the everyday management at a sensitive time when I needed it most.

Being alone for the first time in ten years was a novelty, and as life must go on, there is naturally every possibility that relationships can be formed. Some will not necessarily last a long time, or there might be others whose paths one may cross and whose life one may share for a much longer time but will lead nowhere. As the French phrase would put it so succinctly, *'c'est la vie'*. For some unknown reason, I started writing poetry. It was not because I was alone, but it was simply an expression of understanding life in general and, in particular, myself. As somebody once morbidly pointed out to me on reading my first poem, there was a suggestion of depression, sadness and loss of confidence in all humanity, even suggestions of suicidal intentions. I see it differently.

Aloft Hangs Death

Death it cometh, it's never far,

One body less, there hangs my star.

Hovering, waiting bird of prey, this favour grant, prolong my stay.

That I may love the life I left and offer more to those bereft.

The ones I loved, the ones I knew,

Forget the many but guard the few.

Life of madness, conform and win,

Without belief, the stain of sin,

This subjugation to defeat,

Convention thrives, God keeps his seat.

Creator of life does man perplex

Strength of purpose does Him vex,

Whose counsel gives to those in need,

Less chance to sin, His final deed.

Age and youth.

Helpless old folk, grey and sad,

Gone is the youth that once they had.

Memories linger, all is past,

How much longer must this last?

Misty future, what can you give?

A few more days to breathe and live.

Lucky are those of tender years,

To postpone the thoughts of aged fears.

They all are young, how can they age,

From virile youth to senile sage.

To receive advice, this cannot be,

Such confident youth, all at sea,

Floundering about, their way is lost

Like some small boat, that has been tossed

From rock to rock amid the gale,

Desperate hopes that can only fail.

Just one more hour of this dear life

Extracts last breath, like thrust of knife.

Oh, wretched youth, oh wretched age

At last they've reached the final stage.

Shattering social strata

Drained decanters and sparkling wit,

Artificial prose, they do befit.

Empty glasses, cracked ones too,

Suffer do many, yet far too few.

Fur-lined dresses with silk or mink,

Force those without to stop and think.

How many beads of sweat do pour

To die for those who simply bore.

The idle talk, some foolish whim,

Fat ones get fatter, slim ones slim.

Fatted pheasant in roasting dish,

Diverse choice of exotic fish.

Wines that flow without restraint,

Expressionless face, all caked in paint.

Joyous gathering, all good friends,

Returns the one that he just lends.

Bustling banter, all small talk,

Carriage waiting, too far to walk,

Departing guests bid their farewells,

While arrogant boys do frig around

To be snarled at by some strange hound.

The lights are dim, all is quiet,

One more day, to forget this night.

Lonely Hopeless Captivity.

Prison walls that appear so damp,

Sickening men with chronic cramp,

Rigid rules that offend man's soul,

Menial tasks within this hole.

Strong-armed warders with all their patter,

God's creations, reduced to matter.

Dwindling hopes to solve their plight,

Weak resistance to meet the fight.

Society helps to fight the crimes,

And we the sinners of modern times.

Imposing fines, issuing writs

What can we do, oh hypocrites,

Put them away! Away to jail,

Solves the problem, it cannot fail.

Ten years inside is quite a spell,

To collect one's thoughts within this hell.

Peeling spuds and scrubbing floors,

Mental torment behind closed doors.

Limited space to breathe God's air,

Life is not good, it's just not fair.

The rattle of a passing car,

Brings hope so near, yet oh so far.

The rumbling sound of passing trains,

These tethered souls in rusty chains.

A painful cry within these bars,

Like flies engulfed in sticky jars.

Prisoners saddened and forlorn,

Hope has departed. Life has gone.

You've got a friend.

Happy am I that our paths did cross,

That one girl's gain is another one's loss.

We'll meet again, I know not where,

Those precious moments that we may share

The happy times that we once had

My special friend, she makes me glad

To share her laughs and sometimes tears

To help her with her doubts and fears.

Good luck to her, where'er she goes

One thing for sure, I trust she knows

That all my love to her I send.

It's good to know you've got a friend.

French poetry.

Le livre de la vie est le livre suprême que l'on ne lit qu'une fois
On voudrait revenir à la page où l'on aime,
Mais la page où l'on meure est déjà sous vos doigts.

Translation:

The book of life is the ultimate book that you only read once,

One would like to return to the page where one has loved,

But the page where you die is already in your hands.

Le cimetière est la seule place où l'homme est liberé de ses désirs.

The graveyard is the only place where man is free from his desires.

Forbidden Love.

Forbidden love that thou hast brought
'Gainst thine affections have I fought.
Too weak am I to turn away,
To slam the door or harsh words say.
Our love was kindled in a haze,
Now burns brightly like fire ablaze.
Those gentle lips, so soft and pure
Just one short kiss, my sorrows cure,
Which multiply whene'er we part
With pangs of grief within my heart.
Your love for me is some rare find,
Shouldst I remove it from my mind
And clamber down from this new phase
Or lose my mind within this haze.
This dream that fights within my soul,
Some new horizon is my goal.
Give me your heart, it's ne'er too late
Should this our joy, turn into hate.
To keep our love so warm and true,
Suffer will many, also the few.

Politics

In 1976 I got involved in the anti-colonial struggle in Angola. On one side, there were the Russians and Cubans supporting the People's Movement for Angolan Liberation, and on the other side, there was the Western/American alliance backing the National Union for the Independence of Angola. Ironically both Angolan sides were anti-colonial and wanted to oust all Portuguese influence and involvement in their country. I watched these events on television with interest and was surprised by several reports issued by the main TV channels, revealing that many British ex-soldiers had now become mercenaries, having been promised generous financial rewards and incentives from America. These men were flying to Angola but a report suggested that some of them were leaving without the necessary documentation—i.e. passports. The allegation was that the UK authorities were aware of this, and if these reports were genuine, then it would appear that someone was turning a blind eye so that these potentially well-paid soldiers could reach their destination without too much bureaucratic interference. There was an enormous loss of life affecting not just the British and other international mercenaries but also the Russian and, in particular, the Cuban military divisions. For the British, it would appear that the wrong side won because three British soldiers received the death penalty after a trial in the Zambian capital, Lusaka. All three were shot by firing squad shortly after the verdict was announced. Mr Callaghan, the Prime Minister at the time, pleaded for their acquittal and release but to no avail. On all the news programmes, it was revealed that their bodies were to remain in Angola as the British Government refused to fly these dead bodies home.

I certainly hold no brief or moral support for men who will fight any conflict, especially if the financial reward outweighs the moral principle, but if a man is defending his country against an aggressor through moral principles and not financial gain then I would be more sympathetic to such a just cause. Unfortunately, these men were doing this for money. However, at this point I did get involved. I thought that if it was good enough for these men to be allowed to leave the country as mercenaries, then the least one could do for them and their families would be to return their bodies for dignified burial in the UK.

I have absolutely no connection with the military, but if at the time the Government refused to fly back the deceased personnel, then I felt that somebody should do something about it. I have never bought the *Daily Mail* in my life, but I contacted the editor to say that even though I totally disagree with mercenary soldiers, I believe that these British citizens, whose bodies would be dumped in some obscure graveyard in Angola, should receive the dignity of having their remains returned to their respective families. I sent the newspaper a cheque for £750, which allowed all three bodies to be repatriated in the UK. I received letters of thanks from the families concerned, telling me that they were grateful that my intervention allowed their sons to be buried with dignity.

*   *   *   *

One lunchtime, I walked into a pub and saw Barbara talking to some of her fellow office workers and enjoying a drink together. I had first met her some years ago and not only was she very attractive, but she made me laugh. We had many enjoyable dinners together both in Jersey and St Malo, but somehow, we parted, always amicably and still respecting each other's chosen path. This time was different. I suppose we were more mature, and again, this seemed to work in our favour.

It was the end of another successful season at the hotel, so it was time to think about spending a few days together in France. We drove through the beautiful autumnal colours of Brittany right down to the snowy slopes of St Lary in the Pyrénées. Again, I had to subject her to the ritual pilgrimage of visiting Brive and showing her the little window of the bedroom that I occupied at the age of fourteen. This time was different. I had not seen Jacques since we were both fourteen years of age. I walked from the church steps, crossed the road and peered through the shop window. The shop was busy with customers. At that point I could not believe my eyes. As I was standing outside the window, Jacques appeared along with a customer, who was pointing to a set of frames in the window. Jacques' arm actually touched my sleeve as he was confirming the cost of the lens to the man's request for a price. Somehow, I still could not bring myself to make contact with him. I still had not forgotten how he disappeared for the whole of my stay with his family when he left to go on a cycling tour to Bordeaux. But a strange thing happened after Barbara and I spent our few days together in St Lary. We stayed in the Pyrénées for a week and had a slow drive back through France.

On the return journey, we stopped about thirty kilometres from Brive because I heard of a very good restaurant in a small town where the food was considered by the culinary journalists to be the best in that particular region. In fact, it was a beautiful meal. As we were finishing our coffee, the proprietress asked me what we were doing in the region at that time of the year. I explained my pilgrimage to Brive and how I got to know a family called Mazet through a student exchange visit with their son Jacques.

In French, she said, "You know Jacques Mazet? —he and his wife are our very best friends. You should be there in Brive with him. What will he say when my husband and I tell him that we have actually met you here in our restaurant?"

I said that I thought that he would be surprised and left it at that. When we returned to Jersey, there was a postcard with a photo of Brive on the one side, along with an image of *foie gras* and truffles and on the reverse side was Jacques' handwriting with the word "Why?" written a dozen times in big letters.

However, we renewed our friendship a year later when we stayed in a hotel near their home in Chavagnac and enjoyed a memorable meal together. We spoke about the old times and how good it was to see each other again. We still keep in touch.

A Trip to Egypt

Before opening the hotel for the new season, we had time to take in another holiday. This time it was Egypt. I chose a hotel in El Gouna. It was luxurious with excellent Arab and international food. I must admit that I am not too good at relaxing, doing things like sunbathing or other activities that one associates with holidays. Every morning I would go into the small boutique attached to the hotel and talk to the young manager. Most of the customers were either Dutch, German or French but all used English as a common denominator to make themselves understood and to purchase various items. Everything each customer said I wrote down in English, and the manager very kindly gave me the translation in Arabic, which I learnt like a parrot. Each day I would come back and repeat it to the manager. He was surprised by my progress. Then one day, a really attractive Swiss lady entered the shop with her two pretty daughters. She asked me what I was doing, so I said I like being on holiday, but more importantly, I said I enjoyed learning languages, seeking recipes of local cuisine and learning about Egyptian culture.

She said, "Here in Egypt, they give you total respect, but never, ever will I go back to Tunisia. We went there last year, and the men were horrible. My girls, fourteen and sixteen respectively, were being chased constantly by these over-sexed hooligans."

That did it for me! I always endeavour to see the best in people, so I could not believe that Tunisia was that bad. In the same way that I was influenced to learn Spanish after that chance meeting with the Cockney girls in Spain, I felt an inevitable obligation to go to Tunisia to see what it was like, so there and then I made up my mind and Barbara's to visit the country at the end of the season.

*　　*　　*　　*

In the meantime, a new season arrived. If any bedroom was looking a little jaded, then I would go in and give the whole room a lick of paint. It was good to see so many regular visitors returning year after year. In fact, one year, all the guests actually knew each other from previous visits. We even had a staff versus guests cricket match on St Aubyn's beach. With such a small retinue of staff, some of the guests had to play on our side to balance our lack of players.

One evening I closed the bar around two o'clock and went to my room, feeling exhausted. I had to be up at six-thirty to cook breakfast for sixty guests. Barbara had not been feeling too well so to sleep and relax, she took a Valium tablet. I went to bed and was just about to doze off when I heard the front doorbell ring. It was now two-thirty in the morning. In haste, I just grabbed a bath towel from the bathroom, wrapped it around me, and went to the front entrance, where I saw this smiling couple waving at me. They were a charming couple from Glasgow, but at two-thirty in the morning, even they can lose their charm. They had obviously been out seeing friends and drinking a lot at another hotel. Through the glass door, I tried to admonish them by wagging my finger at them and saying, "You are both very naughty; you have forgotten the door code!"

"I have not," she replied, waving a piece of paper at me upon which the code was written in big letters, her wobbly finger endeavouring to find the metal panel housing the numbers. She put in the code, but it still did not work.

"With respect," I said, shouting through the glass door, "you cannot see what you are doing!"

There I was, with just a towel around me at two-thirty in the morning, lecturing two mature guests on their behaviour.

"I am coming out to show you what you are doing wrong. You've obviously forgotten the code!"

I felt self-conscious dressed as I was, but I opened the door and said, "I will now show you how this damn thing works."

I punched in the code, and to my horror, the door would not budge. They both laughed and said, "We told you so!"

Here I was in the early hours of the morning and unable to gain entry to my own premises. I rang the bell furiously to wake Barbara but to no avail. I think the Valium plus a glass of Sauvignon Blanc must have put her out completely. What could get worse did. As the couple and I were trying to sort out the problem, I saw a police car coming towards the traffic lights. Fortunately, the pair were somewhat physically on the large side, so I pleaded with them to huddle as closely as they could to shield me from the police car, which happened to stop right in front of the hotel entrance, as the lights had just turned red. I pressed the doorbell constantly, and I think that the guest in one of the ground floor rooms must have heard this commotion, as he suddenly appeared in his pyjamas and kindly opened the door. What a night! I thought I could just see the headlines in the *Evening Post*: "Hotelier caught wearing just a towel at the traffic lights".

*   *   *   *

We were watching a BBC cookery programme called *The World of Cooking* in which every country in Europe nominates a competent and talented chef to represent their particular country. The programme that impressed me most was the one specialising in French regional cooking. I watched the programme with interest as the region where the Auberge was situated was unknown to me. The programme revealed the blissful beauty of the region; the special delicacies locally produced, and as a bonus for guests, they could also ski down the nursery slopes.

I wrote a letter to the proprietor of the Auberge and explained quite simply that I had my own busy hotel that closed in November and that I would like to learn more about French regional recipes. "So, could I come and work alongside you?" was my request. I added that I did not want any money and would rent a flat. I said I

150

also wanted to learn about the wines of the region that were a perfect match for the food that he serves. I knew from past travels that in France, every region has its own individual recipes, which quite magically are matched to perfection by the local wine. For example, from St Malo to the Loire Valley, a beautiful *'fruit de mer'* has the Muscadet wine to accompany it, or the Chenin Blanc or a Sauvignon Blanc. Therefore, I wanted to learn more about the recipes and wines of this completely different region of Grenoble and, in particular, the tucked-away village of St Pierre de Chartreuse, where the BBC television series was filmed. After a few weeks, I received a letter from Madame Josette Revest and her husband André, explaining that it would be a pleasure to receive us and for me to work alongside him and learn the regional dishes. He even offered us accommodation.

We were there for five weeks. Once a week, André and I would drive down to the weekly market in Grenoble to buy the beautiful local produce that would last us till the following Monday. It surprised me to see sellers and buyers drinking alcohol from very small thimble-type glasses at five-thirty in the morning. Two major specialities of the region are *'le gratin Dauphinois'*, a potato dish made with garlic, cream and Reblochon cheese and the famous green liqueur called Chartreuse, which is produced by the Carthusian monks at the local monastery. As the climate in winter is particularly cold, I noticed that the dishes served were tasty, very hearty and filling but lacked the delicacy of the more sophisticated tables of France. André cooked a beautiful *'sanglier'* dish which was a boar caught locally by one of his friends in the local hunt. Stag meat *(gigot de chevreuil)* was another beautifully served dish, cooked to perfection by André.

André closed the Auberge every Monday, so Barbara and I invited André and Josette to eat in a restaurant of their choice, La Belle Epoque in Grenoble. This was our way of saying thank you for their kindness. The food in this restaurant was quite sophisticated compared to André's rugged and provincial cooking.

There were all the ingredients that André used, but the presentation was *'nouvelle cuisine'* —no wobbly tables, and the owner poured the wine when she felt like it. When I have paid for the wine, I want it on my table and not isolated four tables away. I was considering how I could use some of my newly acquired recipes on my unsuspecting guests in Jersey, but I knew that I would have to be careful as our regular clientele would not be too keen on change or appreciate sauces made with cream, white wine, garlic and *'Herbes de Provence'*.

After five weeks of working very hard, we became good friends, and to this day we visit each other's home at least once a year. The French have always been chauvinistic with regard to their cheese, but one plus point for me and for the reputation of English cheese is that every time I visit André, the one obligatory rule to secure accommodation in his hotel is to arrive with a block of Stilton cheese. Regarding Yorkshire pudding he still cannot see any logical connection between what he calls a pancake 'crêpe' batter and a delicious joint of Scottish sirloin beef.

For many years, we have eaten the most outstanding food in Caen at La Bourride, which at the time was a two-star Michelin restaurant. The owner, Michel Bruneau, catered for a completely different type of clientele to that of André's local, rugged and traditional cuisine. Michel's cooking was delicate, light and the presentation a work of art—very *'nouvelle cuisine'*. So, one evening, after having eaten a beautifully cooked monkfish, I invited him to our table to have our usual Calvados together. I then asked him if I could work alongside him for a month during the coming winter. He agreed immediately and so the moment we closed our hotel, I returned to Caen to spend a month with him and his talented team. Every morning and evening I was to be found in front of his stove, pencil and paper at the ready, scribbling down new recipes and learning new culinary tricks. After my month with Michel, I moved on to Dinard to the Hotel de la Vallée working with Escoffier chef Guy Cherrier, and there gained more knowledge of French cooking.

With the co-operation of these three talented chefs, André, Michel and Guy, I managed to publish a book in 1995 featuring all of their recipes. The book is entitled *A Cook's Tour of France*.

*   *   *   *

My eldest son, Philip, had always been keen to work with me in the hotel, but this was not the right moment. It would have been too easy to suggest that he make an immediate start, and understandably, he was disappointed that this move did not materialise. It may sound harsh, but my advice, I am sure, was sound. First of all, I said that once achieving the necessary standard stipulated by the Portsmouth College of Hotel Management, he should move back to Jersey and gain experience in one of the group hotels for two or three years and then consider a move to work alongside me. It may possibly portray me as being too harsh and demanding, but as my plan then was to take life easier and perhaps one day withdraw from the daily traumas that kitchen life can bring, I considered the plan I sketched out for Philip was pragmatic. He worked for some years in four hotels within a Channel Island hotel group and gained the necessary experience I insisted upon. This arrangement permitted me to take a back seat and allow me to do all the interesting things I was unable to do during those hectic seasons.

We were very lucky to be introduced to the husband of one of our chambermaids. His name was Castro, and he had already proved himself a talented chef by working at the prestigious Lobster Pot seafood restaurant, which sadly is no more. When he started, I obviously was there working alongside him because I wanted him to know just how my routine worked. Somehow, I hung on as long as I could because there was a sentiment of possessiveness seeing another person in charge of my very wide cooker. Then, after about two weeks, Castro approached me very diplomatically and said in his soft voice, "Graham, you have shown me your routine in the kitchen. I know what you want. I am here to do just that. Why don't you just relax and leave it to me?" I got the message.

He was right but having someone in front of my stove other than me made me feel inadequate, but at the same time grateful because he had the culinary ability I was looking for, and above all, he was a talented and decent man. I remember that moment as if it were yesterday. I did not bother to change out of my kitchen uniform. I just shook his hand, thanked him, and for some unaccountable reason, I walked down the High St in St Helier, still in my chef's outfit and went as far as the Royal Square where there was some political demonstration taking place. I think I was in denial.

We had moved out of the hotel flat and were living just out of town. This move was essential as Philip and his wife, Christine, could then take over my accommodation. His name as a licensee was now printed above the front door, replacing mine. So, with Philip out front in reception and Castro in the kitchen, I knew that I had made a good start to my semi-retirement.

At home in our new accommodation, I looked at my watch, and as the clock struck six o'clock, I felt insecure. I just could not believe that I could be replaced. Call it vanity, pride or even insecurity, I felt disorientated, so I went to the nearest pub. I had a dry Martini, but my mind was elsewhere. I then went home and waited for the phone to ring. When it did, it was Philip's cheerful voice telling me that everything had gone to plan. There were sixty guests in the dining room, and everybody was happy with the food. That put my mind at rest. It took me some weeks to get used to this new situation in my life and as time passed, I began to appreciate more the freedom that this new phase brought me. I started looking forward to enjoying my future without the stress and tribulations of the past. Travel was certainly on the agenda with France being the number one spot.

With the management of the hotel in the safe hands of Philip and Christine and the kitchen supervised by Castro, I thought it was time to take advantage of this new turning point in my life and go to France. Barbara and I took the usual route from St Malo to go south, and no prizes for guessing that we actually spent our first night at the Chapon Fin hotel in Brive. Of course, this brought back happy memories of my stay with the Mazet family when I was fourteen. I was happy then and a lot happier now. The next day we drove into new territory, into the 'département' of Aude to the town of Lézingnan Corbières. This is the region of France where the persecuted Cathars were judged to be dissidents and heretics by Rome and the Catholic Church universally, and they did everything both morally and physically to crush this particular form of Christianity.

We drove on to the beautiful town of Lagrasse, had lunch beginning with snails in garlic butter followed by sweetbreads. Afterwards we drove on without any particular destination in mind. We came to some crossroads and I was on the point of driving straight on when Barbara suggested turning left, which I did. This decision would cause me twelve years of legal frustration but more of that later. We arrived ten minutes later in the small village of Fabrezan, and we stayed there in the Hôtel des Souquets for three nights. We liked the region and thought it would be nice to find somewhere to rent instead of spending our time in hotels. The proprietress, Diane, said she had a property available that we could rent. It was just around the corner from the hotel and had everything we were looking for. The rent was reasonable, and the small village had just one hotel, one chemist, one newsagent, two bars and one lawyer's office. We told Diane that we would rent the house for a year. That would give us the time to look for a property to buy, should we decide to stay in this region. I was extremely happy. The hotel in Jersey was constantly full. It was being well-managed by Philip with the capable support of his wife, and the kitchen was in the safe hands of Castro. What could go wrong? Well, it did in a big way.

From the rented house, we would often drive to Lagrasse, because the restaurant and bar both had a great atmosphere, the food was excellent and the staff welcoming. On the way to Lagrasse, there is an even smaller village called Ribaute. I slowed down to read and get a better look at a flimsy sign fluttering in the breeze advertising a piece of land for sale just set back off the road. We noted the estate agent's address and went to their office. They referred us to the mayor, who informed us that the land had been passed for the construction of either one very large house or two smaller ones. I liked the challenge of having a piece of land with such potential and approved for construction by the mayor. This was the blank canvas on which we could trace and outline a new beginning to our life in France, either by constructing a traditional village house or by building two homes, selling one and living in the other. The latter appealed more to the financial machinations of my mind.

"Ça vous plaît?" asked the wrinkly-faced Mayor of Ribaute, looking at us with a twinkle in his eye.

"Oui, ça nous plaît beaucoup," I responded, saying that I have decided to buy this plot of land.

He asked me if I had my chequebook with me. I said I had not but that I would go back to the house and get it. He said he would come with us in the car so that he could introduce me to the Notaire and finalise the purchase. He told me that his lawyer, Maître Oustric, would act for me and also for the village of Ribaute. I felt that I needed to know more about this lawyer as he was acting for both parties.

The mayor told me that he was a fine lawyer who would finalise the purchase. All three of us drove to the Notaire's office. Barbara went to the house to get my chequebook, and a few minutes later, she joined us in the lawyer's study. At this point in time, all the lawyer wanted was 10% of the purchase price to establish the *'compromis de vente'*—a pre-sale agreement—which I paid immediately. When the remaining 90% would be paid, that would establish an *'acte de vente authentique'* —the final agreement, which I was prepared to pay there and then. However, the 10% deposit means that neither side can back out without paying hefty penalties. The lawyer's wife, Madame Oustric, got me to sign the documentation that Monsieur Oustric had drawn up for me. We shook hands, and the lawyer, his wife and then the mayor congratulated us on our purchase and wished us *"bonne continuation"*. "You now own your own little corner of France," said the mayor.

The lawyer's son saw us heading off to one of the two bars in the village and asked if he could join us. We spent a good hour together telling him our plans for this large piece of land. Once again, we received more congratulations from him. I had to attend to some business in Jersey and wanted the sale completed before I left. I had also sought the services of an architect who was very encouraged by my enthusiasm in developing this building plot. Before leaving for Jersey, I must have visited the lawyer's office six times to complete the official sale of paying off the 90% outstanding. He was either too busy to see me or he was with a client. I cornered him the day before leaving when I was buying the local newspaper and saw him standing outside his office.

"Monsieur Anderson, on n'est pas pressé!" No, he certainly was not in a hurry, but I was, and I told him that I wanted the sale completed and settled on my return.

"Oui, je m'en occuperai," he said, assuring me that he would take care of it. We returned to Jersey, and after a few days, I received a phone call that shocked me. At the time of the call, I was up to my eyes in work, painting the skirting boards along the corridors. I put down my brush and heard the gravelly voice of Maître Oustric. He said he was very sorry but had made a big mistake and had accidentally sold my land to a third party. "So, what I'll do is to send you a cheque for the 10% you paid, and that will settle the matter." Obviously, all this was spoken in French, and during the call, he used the slang terminology, *"J'ai fait une boulette"* which means "I have made a complete and utter balls-up of this matter".

Now it was my turn. "My dear Maître Oustric, I will not accept your offer to return my 10% deposit. I will give you one last chance to return the land to my ownership. We have a contract with both our names on it and signed by us both. I thought I was dealing with a man of principal and honour. I was wrong."

"Sorry," he went on, "but it is too late; somebody else has bought it."

"In that case, I shall take immediate legal action against you," I replied and put down the phone.

My next task was to look for an honourable lawyer to take on my case. It came about in a rather strange way. I have certainly met some very strange people in my lifetime, but perhaps none stranger than Marcel. One day I was introduced to him via a friend who met him by chance at a petrol station. My friend mentioned to him, in passing, that I needed legal advice from a lawyer regarding my loss of land in Ribaute. Marcel knew the area well and also said that he had an excellent lawyer in Narbonne. So, I arranged to meet Marcel. This is the perfect example of totally disagreeing with a person politically, even socially but at the same time, it did not stop me liking him. First of all, he, along with his family, had been lifelong members of the Communist Party and suddenly with a complete change of direction, he joined Madame Le Pen's right-wing National Front Party and became an extremist, hating all foreigners—except for, it seems, Barbara and myself.

To add to this confusion, he was living with the most charming of ladies, a Jewish widow who cooked some of the most magnificent food I have ever tasted. *Mon Dieu*—I certainly meet them! Marcel made an appointment with his lawyer in Narbonne to look into my case. We arrived at around two-thirty in the afternoon; I explained what had happened with my land to Maître Claude Calvet, and he thought I had a very strong case but gave me a warning, in his own words, "A foreign person accusing a French lawyer of a misdemeanour in a French court would in itself be a challenge to the system". He said he would willingly take on my case.

The first thing I did was to leave Fabrezan and the rented house and amicably discontinued the lease. We could not stay a day longer as I would have bumped into my adversary either in the newsagents, the chemist's or in one of the two bars. We drove down to Argelès-sur-mer, a beautiful area of the Pyrénées Orientales, and rented a flat with a sea view. My newly acquired political deviant friend, Marcel, went to Fabrezan with his large van and trailer and brought all our belongings back to our new address. We thanked him, took him out for a meal, settled up with him and then he drove back to his house near Lézignan-Corbières.

The first court hearing took place in *'le Tribunal de Narbonne'*. The process was not very long, and it was some time before the result was announced. I opened Maître Calvet's letter and with absolute joy, I shouted, "We've won!"

It was only a few days later that we received another letter from Maître Calvet informing us that my adversary was going to appeal the decision. I phoned my lawyer to thank him for his efforts and then he told me something quite remarkable. He said, "Mr Anderson, you know you bought the land on the Thursday, well your land was sold to a developer in Narbonne for three times the price the following day."

My adversary appealed at 'La Cour de Cassation' in Montpellier and, surprisingly, the decision went in his favour, but I was not finished with him yet. My lawyer, Maître Calvet, put in an appeal on my behalf in the High Court in Paris, and we won our case. Surprisingly my opponent appealed this decision and, with one more throw of the dice, took his case – this time finally – to the Appeal Court in Toulouse, where once more, the verdict went in my favour. There was nowhere else for him to go, and I was glad that the Court rejected my adversary's appeal and granted me victory. All together, it took twelve years to be awarded 14,000 euros. Certainly, with all the travelling costs, hotels, petrol, restaurants and ancillary expenses it may seem to some people that it was not worth bothering about, but to me it was a matter of principle and in the end, I won.

Our legal battle in Languedoc - Roussillon, France.

The **Connexion** May 2005

COUPLE WIN 12-YEAR FIGHT OVER LOST LAND

Lawyer re-sold Languedoc plot without their knowledge

FOLLOWING a marathon legal battle, Graham Anderson and Barbara Taylor have finally received compensation for the loss of a building plot they tried to buy in 1993, which the lawyer handling the transaction re-sold without informing them.

The land in the village of Ribaute (Aude) was sold on again three months later for three times more than the original price.

The couple, who own a hotel in Jersey, were awarded €14,000 at a final appeal court ruling in Toulouse. That sum includes the deposit paid for the land although, as Mr Anderson pointed out, the couple have spent much more on travel and accommodation in their efforts to secure victory.

"It was the principle that drove us to pursue the case. I couldn't bear the fact that the lawyer had misled us," said Mr Anderson. After agreeing a price for the land directly with the mayor of Ribaute, the couple had obtained a provisional sales agreement and paid the required deposit. The mayor reportedly told them, "You now own a little corner of France."

However, months went by without the completion of the sale despite pressure from Mr Anderson. In March 1994, the lawyer telephoned to say he had made "a serious mistake" and had re-sold the land to an estate agency in Narbonne.

A property search revealed that the plot was sold again soon after for three times more than the original price.

Refusing to accept their deposit back, the Jersey couple took the lawyer to court in Narbonne and won. He then appealed the ruling in Montpellier, where it was reversed and the couple ordered to pay costs. Next they took the case to the Court of Appeal in Paris and once again secured victory. Not content, the lawyer lodged a further appeal in Toulouse.

Late last year, the original ruling was reconfirmed, and the couple were finally vindicated and awarded compensation.

While Mr Anderson believes that he and his partner were "unlucky", he told *The Connexion*, "Other people should be warned that buying property in France is not always easy. We decided not to let this pass, but the average person may well have given up and gone home." A fluent French speaker, Mr Anderson recommended that those who do not speak the language well should have important documents translated.

Also for an Englishman to bring a French lawyer to heel in a French court was in the words of my lawyer *"une réussite formidable"* —a fantastic victory.

*   *   *   *

As fate would have it, we were very happy with our latest move to Argelès, and even though we suffered years of legal conflict and our plans were thwarted, it turned out to be to our advantage. We rented for two further years an apartment near the beach. As was usual for our Friday night out, we went to our favourite restaurant in the town of Argelès, Relais de La Massane. As I parked the car in front of the restaurant, I noticed that a village house next to the restaurant was for sale and noted that the estate agency was Agence de la Gare. We enjoyed our meal and had a last digestif with the owners.

The next day I contacted the agency and arranged for a visit to view the village house that same day. I was aware that it was in desperate need of being totally renovated to make it a viable project, but it was a charming two-hundred-year-old village house full of potential, but more importantly, it would be our home. We agreed on the price, and along with the estate agent, we all went to the lawyer's office, signed the contract, and I handed over the cheque.

We knew quite a few of the local tradesmen, as they would often pop into one of the several bars in town for their Pastis before going home to their family. In this way, we put together a good team. They said it would take a good few months to complete. We were so proud. Well, even if it was not Brive, we couldn't have been happier. At last, we had bought our first house in the Pyrénées, but like any project in France, it would have its moments of despair.

Our beautiful but shabby *'maison de village'*, once renovated from a neglected old ruin into something resembling a cosy and permanent home, would make us both feel proud and part of the Catalan community. So, putting together a reliable team of tradesmen was the next challenge. The Catalan man is a very proud person. Here the accent can be quite different from the rest of France, and when I first arrived in this village, I would often ask someone the sensitive question, "Are you French?" and the terse answer was delivered with a corrective response, *"Non, je suis Catalan! Peut-être après ça, français !"* Catalan first and French a poor second.

From Argelès to the Spanish border at Le Perthus is a twenty-five-minute journey by car, but doing the same trip in July could take up to two hours with the conglomeration of traffic and their occupants seeking all the cheap, duty-free cigarettes, alcohol, petrol and leather goods that would cost a great deal more in France. I discovered a very interesting dish across the border in La Jonquera, in a simple back-street restaurant, Bar 2000, where the mixture of Spanish and Catalan culture produced the dish of *'Conejo con caracoles'*—a dish of rabbit with two dozen snails served in a red wine sauce with onions, carrots, tomatoes, the liver of the rabbit and garlic. At first, I just did not think it would work as a classic dish, but it does. Every time we go there, I make sure it is on the menu before I enter. Unfortunately, the other restaurant where this dish was served and was perhaps the best in La Jonquera – the Artigas– is now closed permanently due to the father dying and subsequent family members squabbling over future management and ownership.

*   *   *   *

A French worker has a completely different attitude to his counterpart in the UK when it is a question of food. So often in Jersey, I have seen workers stop for lunch at about one o'clock, and this consisted of ham or cheese sandwiches from a plastic box accompanied by a thermos flask containing tea or coffee. This would take him about half an hour to satisfy his hunger before returning to whatever he was doing before this average lunch interfered with his work. So, every day we went to our *'maison de village'* just to see how work was progressing and to see if our new kitchen had been delivered by Schmidt, the kitchen specialists. We arrived about lunch time, just before twelve-thirty and parked right outside. The drive from the flat only took about fifteen minutes. As I opened the car door, I suddenly received the full flush of sizzling garlic and onions coming from my property. There was absolutely no noise coming from the building, so I assumed the workers must have disappeared to Maria's bar, just up the concrete steps that led to the place favoured by the workers looking for a sly drink. As I got closer to my front door, the smell of garlic, parsely and melted butter *(persillade)* became even more intense. On entering the hallway, the first room you see is the one on the left, which officially is the garage, but which will become a bedroom with a private suite. The door was ajar. I looked around in search of life or anyone to let me know how work was progressing. I then heard voices. They must have heard me opening the door. On seeing me they were polite and greeted us with handshakes. There was Isadore, the electrician and a fellow worker who greeted me warmly. But it was what I saw that intrigued me. They had obviously just finished their lunch and were about to recommence their work. On the floor of the garage was a portable gas ring with a tiny gas cylinder attached; on top was a frying pan, with the excess fat from an entrecote piece of steak pushed to one side and a pack of Normandy butter on a sideboard. Nearby was a half-empty Pastis bottle, an empty carafe of red wine, two dirty plates and glasses, the outer leaves of several cloves of garlic and a garlic crusher. Their work was first-class, so if this was the result of fine dining at work, then I was all in favour.

I know that the French pay great attention to the bedroom and the kitchen, in which order of preference, I am not too sure, but the carpenter Jean-Pierre kept going on about making sure that these two important aspects of French life received his total and undivided attention and he saw to it that these two rooms would be completed before all the other necessary alterations to the other rooms. So, I agreed to his plan of completing these two rooms first, before all others.

I soon discovered his logic in organising my house to fit in with his plans. It was the beginning of July when the plumbers, plasterers and electricians started work at 26 Rue Marcellin Albert. The weather was perfect, hot but not too oppressive. We were naturally overjoyed with the progress so far, but we were anxiously waiting for completion so that we could have the house to ourselves. We still made our daily visits just to see what progress had been made. But this day was different because we had been invited to lunch by our neighbours, André and Liliane, from the adjoining apartment block to celebrate their wedding anniversary. We had a truly memorable lunch consisting of foie gras followed by seabass with a *'beurre blanc'* sauce followed by a mountain of local cheeses and crusty *'pain de campagne'*. I have always had a policy of never drinking and driving, so as it was a special day, we took a taxi to and from the restaurant. At the time, I thought how wonderful life was. Back in Jersey, Philip and Christine were looking after the hotel, and here we were in the South of France, having done justice to a sensational meal. The owner of the restaurant delayed our departure by offering us *"un digestif de Banyuls"*. We felt on top of the world. We called a taxi and asked the driver to stop outside our house for five minutes while we went inside to see what progress had been made.

It was three-thirty in the afternoon when we arrived at the house. Instinctively, I knew something was wrong. The exterior garage doors, normally open, were bolted and looking up at the windows, I saw all the shutters were firmly closed. With great trepidation, I opened the front door, but there was nobody there. No plumber, no electrician, no carpenter, no plasterer and no smell of garlic. We went upstairs to the lounge and opened the shutters to let the light in. I then saw a note on the dining room table from the foreman. *"On est parti pour nos vacances annuelles, à bientôt à trois semaines, donc"*. A simple message, straight to the point, but I was in shock. They'll be back in three weeks when obviously the weather will be cooler for them to continue their work. I was angry, so we told the taxi driver not to wait for us as we both needed another drink. We went up the concrete steps and a minute later, I explained our ordeal to Maria. She could see my anger but with a shrug, she said, *"Mais c'est normal, il fait trop chaud pour travailler, donc on passe un mois ou plus dans les collines ou la température est plus agréable."*

She agreed. It was too hot to work.

Maria was not surprised because as she explained most workers seek a cooler temperature in the hills and mountains of the Pyrénées to escape the high temperatures in August and then return normally three weeks or a month later when it is cooler to start work again. She said there was no point in hiring other builders as they all disappear to the hills to avoid the heat. She thought we were lucky because they would only be away three weeks instead of four. She knew them all as customers and told me to calm down and not to worry.

In the taxi going back to our flat, we discussed the forthcoming visit of two people from England we had met on holiday in Egypt. A week previously, we had received an animated phone call from the husband saying how thrilled he was, because he got a fabulous price for two tickets from Manchester to Girona in Spain. Well it would have been better for us had he booked the trip to Perpignan Airport which is only thirty-five minutes away from Argelès. Maybe it was the wine or perhaps sarcasm on my part, but I said how nice it will be to drive the two-hour journey to Girona and try to appreciate our friends' luck in finding such a bargain flight. After that experience, I laid down the law to all prospective future visitors. If anyone wishes to visit us, they do not fly to Girona, Montpellier or Toulouse. If they cannot make it to Perpignan, my advice is to stay home.

I was still morosely going on about the builders disappearing during the month of August. I started saying that this could never happen in England. I was adding to my grief by moaning about French manners in supermarkets and the way in which they jump the queue. Three times it has happened to me and even though it was my turn on each occasion, I stood back and waved my hand in the regal manner of a courtier and said, *"Après vous Madame, parce qu' en Angleterre nous avons toujours le respect pour la femme."* On each occasion, it was always a woman who pushed in. I always received a thank you and a big smile when they misinterpreted my sarcasm for gallantry, after my sentence saying that an Englishman always gives respect to a lady.

Some other mannerisms of the French are highly amusing. For instance, whenever I have stopped the car to ask directions or any simple question, and they do not know the answer, there is only one response possible. The person will look vaguely in an upward direction with eyes following this movement towards the heavens, blink the eyes, purse the lips, raise both outstretched hands at an equal distance above both shoulders in a surrender position, and with both lips pursed tightly will blow forth a verbal raspberry. No other mannerism is possible.

Another facial peculiarity is when a Frenchman tells you that someone is totally broke, is skint and has not got a penny or a euro to his name. He will get the thumbnail of his right hand and neatly place it under one of his upper top teeth, and then he will release the thumb and nail in a forward movement making a clicking noise. I saw this procedure once when the man carrying out this procedure forgot that he had a set of dentures. I suppose you could say that it just came out in conversation!

Another favourite is expressing how expensive something is. All the fingers of the right hand are splayed about chest high, but the thumb must be in an upright and almost vertical position. Then the whole ensemble is shaken at least three times as if the person is suffering with some nervous ailment or a twitch associated with alcoholism. I learnt a great deal of these movements from the artisans I employed at my house.

So, Maria's advice was sound. Wait until the workers return and the job is completed, and do not try to replace the workers otherwise, in such a small community, the word would go around that the English are the proverbial *'emmerdeurs'* and not to be trusted. It was testing my patience because to interfere with their summer siesta in the hills and valleys of the Pyrénées would be considered a betrayal, pulling them away from one of the many mountain bars where they were waiting for the baking summer temperatures in Argelès to subside, and then to be replaced by the infernal Tramontane. This is the very strong wind that can knock people off their feet. It is said to cause deep depression, and Catalan people are convinced that there is a serious connection between this fierce tempest and the suicide rate in the Languedoc-Roussillon region.

So, for the time being, it was just a matter of waiting. Logically the bedroom was complete and, just as important, the kitchen was fully functional, so we could sleep and eat amongst the rest of this chaos and just wait for the builders to honour us with their presence. When they did return, I must admit they worked with renewed enthusiasm. With this Pyrenean pilgrimage done and dusted for another year, I noticed that most of the workers had put on a few extra kilos in weight, especially around the waist department. They did work well, and the job was finished to perfection. With the interior work completed, there was just the outside plastering and painting to finish off to complete the whole contract.

The next day a really pleasant Arab man named Karim, originally from Morocco, arrived with an array of plastering material, filler, brushes and cream paint for the walls and blue paint for the shutters. He started work standing on an antiquated mechanism that resembled a scaffold. However, it looked safe, and he finished in record time without incurring any injury to himself or the scaffold. After dismantling this complicated but effective entanglement, he shook my hand and said, *"Ma'as-salama"*— goodbye. I foolishly offered him a Pastis but of course, he replied with courtesy and said that he was a Muslim and did not drink alcohol. I did ask him about the recipe for couscous, and the moment he heard this magical word, he insisted that Barbara and I should go to his home the following Sunday and his wife would show me how to make the perfect couscous. We went to his home in Perpignan, avoided the herd of Pitbull terriers, thankfully all chained up in the yard, and went into the house to enjoy Moroccan hospitality from Karim, his wife and daughter. I also learnt how to make the perfect couscous. On the way out we bypassed the savage-looking beasts who looked at us as potential dinner.

Slowly but surely, the work on the house was finally completed during the first week of October. All the tradesmen came into the sparkling kitchen on the first floor and as it was just before lunch, I offered them a gin and tonic, but being Catalan and chauvinistic, they said they could see a bottle of Banyuls on my shelf, so I poured them a glass each. Had we been in Marseille, and not Catalan country, it would automatically have been Pastis, but these were proud people—Catalonia first France a poor second.

We thanked them for their work, and they all disappeared up the concrete steps that inevitably lead to Maria's bar, where I suspect they would be spending some of the money I had just given them. The house was sparkling, ceilings, walls in fact everything inside was pure white and gleaming with that comforting smell of fresh paint. After seeing the men off, we went upstairs to the lounge-cum-kitchen and finally climbed up to the sun terrace, a massive area above the two bedrooms and looked around at our new and shining possession. We were ecstatic with the result. We went downstairs into the lounge to fill two glasses from a *'cubis'*—red wine in a box. I do not think I had ever tasted wine so fruity and smooth, but of course, it was our moment to celebrate.

My son phoned to say that the hotel was full, the bar extremely busy and the staff very happy. As I drank my wine, looking out over the nearby river, I wondered what on earth could spoil this moment of joy. Well, something did. The fierce and unrelenting Tramontane started to make its way from its starting point in the Pyrénées, across the locally worshipped Mount Canigou, and blow it did. We knew that it was responsible for a certain amount of damage and inconvenience every year, but this time, according to locals, it was different. Before I bought the house, I specifically asked Jean-Charles, the estate agent, if the property was subject to flooding, having already noticed what I would call a mere stream across the road, directly opposite the house. He told me he had lived the best part of his youth in the adjoining property and had never seen anything untoward regarding flooding.

As a precaution I moved my BMW to an area higher up along the road just below a bridge that was higher than the lower strip of land in front of the house. We had been so busy that we missed out on our usual trip to the supermarket in Saint André, but I thought I could easily walk to the mini-supermarket in the centre of Argelès later that day. The shutters started to rattle, and the wind seemed to gather strength. Suddenly it took off. I have never in my life seen rain or heard the noise of the wind like this. Suddenly what was basically an empty dried-up stream became in minutes a fast-flowing river, and fill up it did. From the window, I watched this river expand its flow and creep menacingly in the direction of our front door. This torrential rain went on relentlessly for hours and what started as a stream now turned into a gushing river covering cars that were casually parked between our house and the next-door restaurant. I went downstairs and could see through the thick glass panel of the front door that the height of the water had reached a foot, but somehow no water had, as yet, penetrated the garage or the hallway. The rain would just not stop. The level of the water was getting higher and higher. What I did next defies all logic and now seems quite stupid. I opened the front door, and with the pressure of water building up, I was catapulted at least ten feet to finish up in a position of being mildly injured at the bottom of the staircase. The water gushed into the hallway and overflowed into the garage, and started getting higher. I promptly decided that somehow, I must close the front door to stop more water from coming in. I was knee-deep in water and found that one of the hinges had been ripped off with the pressure of opening the door. I went upstairs, soaking wet and started worrying about some of the contents in the garage, especially a recently bought French dresser from Monsieur Meuble in Perpignan. We used the garage basically as a storeroom and occasionally as a spare bedroom for friends and family to stay in.

We looked out of the window and what used to be a dried-up river, was now in full flow. From left to right there were dustbins floating on the surface and two cars that had been left by people who perhaps went to do some shopping, were now completely covered by water. With nothing in the fridge, we decided to have a glass of wine to calm our nerves. There was nothing more we could do. With the door off its hinge there was no way anybody could enter the house as we had wrought-iron outer doors locked for security.

The next day, I went downstairs to open the outer gates and found that they were congealed with black mud. Outside was similar. Slippery mud; the water had now receded and found its own level. I then walked to see if my car had suffered any damage on the slightly higher ground. It was completely covered in slime and mud and was embedded in the trunk of a plane tree and would not start. The BMW garage in Perpignan towed the car away and, after three days, brought it back with the advice that it should be sold the moment we return home to Jersey. It seemed to go as well as ever, but I thought seriously about the advice he gave me.

The next day Jean-Charles came sheepishly to our front door without the top hinge to express his sorrow at what had happened on our first day of moving in and being free from builders. He held a copy of the local newspaper *L'Indépendant* in his hand and showed me the front page. It was the story of a young girl who was driving her small Renault car in the nearby village of Sorède, and, finding herself driving into a torrent of rising water, she panicked and decided to get out of her car. Unfortunately, a manhole cover had floated away, and in trying to escape, she was sucked down the manhole and sadly drowned.

*　　　*　　　*　　　*

Having a base in France was ideal for our numerous trips to the Spanish border, but being so ideally situated, there were other European countries that were now accessible. A country I had never visited was Portugal. Having employed so many Portuguese workers in the hotel made me think how beautiful it would be if only I could converse with them in their own language. They really are the most hard-working community one could ever wish for, but their interest and command of English was, at times, a little shaky and this made communication somewhat harder. I did what I have always done when I want to learn a language. With the hotel closed during the winter, I bought a Linguaphone Portuguese language course and started studying and repeating like a parrot what I heard on the cassette. It was not just a few minutes here and there but a solid battering of the eardrums, which meant five hours' intense study and repetition of everyday vocabulary. I even went to sleep with earplugs bellowing out the language.

For example, a young child up to the age of three or four has little or no knowledge of the written word or how to interpret it. It is the ear that picks up repetitive phrases, and along with repetition and emphasis on its application, a child will respond using the very words he or she has just heard even though their ability to write those same words would be more than a challenge. Call it parrot-fashion, but I have found that, when for instance, I have given English lessons to French students, and a certain word forms a mental block, I will oblige the student to repeat that particular word six times and after that write it down, study it and think of nothing else until perfection is reached.

I then decided that a trip to Portugal was the only answer to my linguistic search for improving my knowledge of the language. I know people say that it should be easy having already mastered Spanish and indeed, there are similarities, but there are also many discrepancies. Why is a frying pan *'sartén'* in Spanish and *'frigideira'* in Portuguese? Sounds more like a fridge! I find Spanish the more delicate and musical of the two languages, whereas even similar words in Portuguese are pronounced very differently with what I would call an eternal lisp when it comes to pronouncing the letter "s".

We started our journey from our base in Argelès and drove in the direction of Lourdes in the Hautes Pyrénées region in order to arrive at the Spanish border town of St Jean de Luz. We crossed into Spain at Hendaye and drove non-stop across Northern Spain and passed through Ferral, famous or perhaps infamous as the birthplace of General Franco. From there, we drove across the border through the non-commercial but nevertheless beautiful scenery of the North-West region of Portugal. Eventually, just as it was getting dark, I saw a sign displaying the direction, Figueira da Foz. I was very tired after this long drive and, I simply had to stop and find some hotel for the night. We checked into a simple *'pousada'* and found a little restaurant that served us a dish that I will always remember due to the unusual combination of meat and shellfish. It was *'costeleta de porco al alentejo'*. It was the first time ever I had eaten a pork chop served with clams on the same plate plus a very light sauce. Unusual but delicious. The next day I went into a shop adjacent to the hotel and spoke to the owner in a faltering Portuguese sentence that I had learnt like the proverbial parrot. I asked her if she knew of anyone in the town who could give me lessons in Portuguese. The lady spoke reasonably good English and, with a smile on her face, said there was a lady teacher in Rua da Fonte, a lecturer in English at the University of Coimbra. Her name was Fernanda Borges Pestana, and she gave private tuition. She wrote down the lady's name and address on the back of a parking ticket, so I immediately went to see her.

I rang the bell, and a lady of a certain age opened the door and immediately I knew she was the right person to teach me the language. University trained, years of experience and excellent English, she had a big smile, and in answer to my question as to when I could commence my first lesson, she simply said, "Would you like to start now?"

Without thinking, I said, "Yes, I would like that very much."

"Well then, come inside. First of all, we'll have a cup of coffee and discuss matters."

I explained the reason for my wanting to learn Portuguese and said that I employed quite a few staff who come from the island of Madeira and that out of respect for them, I would like to speak to them and understand what they are saying in their own language.

After all, I said jokingly, they could be talking about me and saying what a horrible employer I was. If so, I would like to know why.

"No, you seem like a nice man to me. Let's start talking Portuguese," she said.

She was reasonably pleased with my efforts in speaking the language but said, "You'll need more than just that if you want to succeed."

What I had perfected and repeated to her was, "*Se faz favour, pode-me trazer dois copos de vinho da casa?*"—said to a barman, meaning 'can you bring me two glasses of house wine?' which is really useful when the car has a flat tyre!

I started my course there and then. We discussed terms, which I agreed to immediately. She was absolutely fantastic, not just as a communicator of language but also as a genuine person. Two hours every day was the arrangement for a period of five weeks. She gave me homework which I did conscientiously. Obviously, applying what I already knew, in addition to what I learned every day, was an asset whenever we went out to bars, *cafés* and restaurants. This is where the basic, everyday language is spoken and where most people will help you if they see that you are making an effort to speak their language. In fact, they are flattered because with English being the commercial language of the world, why should an Englishman want to learn their language, which, in the pecking order, comes well after other Latin languages such as French, Spanish or Italian?

Fernanda and her husband Estêvão said goodbye to us after five weeks of intense study. We hadn't just made two very good friends, but I had accomplished my mission to improve my knowledge of the language. I hadn't totally achieved my ambition of understanding the other aspect of the Portuguese language, and that was the Portuguese spoken in Brazil. So, a year after my crash course with Fernanda, I jumped on a Tap Air flight to Rio da Janeiro with Barbara. Once there, I enrolled as a student in Ipanema at the Berlitz School of Languages. I think that because Brazil is the only major country in South America where Portuguese is spoken, the language has been influenced by the surrounding countries where Spanish is the predominant language, and when Brazilians speak, to my ear, it sounds like the musical version of Spanish being spoken, not sounding like the Portuguese spoken in Europe. The one big mistake I made was the following, which shows that one word in European Portuguese can have a completely different meaning in Brazil. Referring to a woman in Lisbon the correct word is *"rapariga"* but if used, as I did when referring to a lady in Copacabana, then the meaning is derogatory and means a very loose woman morally. I spent two weeks at the Berlitz and on the last day was handed my certificate of proficiency. After that, I thought I would be able to find out if my Portuguese staff were talking about me!

Just to continue my enthusiasm and interest in learning languages, I decided to learn Italian. So, a year after Brazil, we were back in our house in France and organising a route for our journey to Italy. The journey from Argelès took us through Narbonne, Montpellier, Toulon, Monaco, and finally, we crossed the border town of Menton and then we were in Italy. We drove past San Remo and finished up in the seaside town of Poggia Caiano. We were staying in a lovely hotel where the food was excellent, along with that of all the other restaurants we visited. In the hotel, there was a beautiful Italian language teacher who was giving lessons to an Indian family who were involved in the clothing industry locally. The teacher's name was also Barbara, and so I asked her if I could start a course of Italian with her. We spent two hours together daily speaking the colloquial language of everyday necessities, such as ordering food and drinks in bars and restaurants, shopping together, booking a hotel room and just general conversation. I appreciate that every language has a certain beauty, but for me, Italian is the most artistic and musical-sounding language, interspersed with effervescent and mellifluous sounds that no other language can match. The singing voices of Pavarotti and Bocelli come to mind, even when merely sitting in a café ordering cappuccinos and listening to the simple conversation of a customer chatting to the waiter or simply ordering a coffee. Such is the beauty of this magical language. Fortunately, we have a Sicilian, Nino, in our family, so whenever I need a linguistic hand, he is always there to help me and correct my mistakes.

*　　*　　*　　*

I wrote earlier about a Swiss lady I encountered in a hotel souvenir shop in Egypt who made the most critical and derogatory remarks about the Tunisian people—in particular the men, whom she said were lecherous and constantly chasing after her two young daughters who would be in danger if left in their company. I have always thought that generalisations are dangerous and that all people, irrespective of their background, culture or language, have the same desires to be free, both politically and domestically, and to give and receive love and affection. The following is a simple but beautiful quotation by the French philosophical and literary artist Gustave Flaubert which says that a person with a kind heart can be universally loved.

"Le Coeur est le citoyen de tous les pays."

Of all the countries I have visited, I sincerely believe that where I have encountered abject poverty, the people are more caring and courteous than most economically rich and developed countries. Strangely enough, the more poverty-stricken the people are, the stronger their faith, whichever religion they were born into or whichever religion they have adopted. Peculiarly enough, I have often been influenced, decision wise, by people with whom I disagree, so the Swiss lady with her views on Tunisian men made me want to go and visit the country, just to see if I could prove her wrong.

We arrived at the Zodiac Hotel in Hammamet Yasmine and were delighted with the warm and welcoming start we received at reception. Perhaps the Swiss lady's views were still ringing in my ears when a host of various nationalities were checking in about the same time. I was looking, too closely, perhaps at any deviant behaviour from the male staff towards some of the attractive women arrivals. They were all behaving like gentlemen, pouring orange juice, carrying suitcases and being as helpful as one would expect them to be. The manager personally handed us two glasses of orange juice as a welcoming gesture plus a small dish of sweet dates and some black olives. After that, our bags were carried up to our room, which was beautifully furnished and overlooking the swimming pool. So far, so good. The reception staff had a good knowledge of French, which would be, for them, a good standby, should they not be able to find the right word in English.

Contrary to most people's belief, the Tunisians are not Arabs, even though Arabic is the official language of the country. They are in fact Berbers. So, no prizes for what happened next. Yes, I went to reception and asked the Manager if there was a school in Hammamet where I could learn Arabic. He said there was *L'Ecole de la langue Arabe* in Hammamet. The next day I didn't bother with breakfast but hailed one of the many taxis whizzing along the road in front of the hotel and told the driver to take me to the school.

I arrived at the school's reception desk, and there to greet me was a man who would become one of my best friends ever. He was skinny, with an enormous smile on his face. He had two dark strips of hair on either side of his head and not so much on top. It just so happened that he was the greatest Anglophile you could ever wish to meet. He knew every song and every word of the lyrics written by the Beatles. Unfortunately, he thought he could sing like John Lennon or Paul McCartney, but this was a mistake! He knew all the one-liners by Rowan Atkinson, John Cleese and practically the whole scripts of Monty Python. My teacher's name was Wahid Ajabi, but he preferred to be known as Woody because he did resemble Woody Allen.

I got off to the perfect start, because when a teacher can speak English as well as Wahid, it makes translation and the search for

177

idiomatic synthesis that much easier when looking for the correct interpretation— *'le mot juste'*.

"Well Graham, would you like to learn Tunisian Arabic or Classical Arabic?"

"Wahid, I didn't know there were two types of Arabic, but I want to be understood in every Arab country I go to, so I do not see the point in learning a language that is confined to just one people and one country."

He agreed and led me into a classroom for my first individual lesson to find out just how much I knew. I brought with me a Berlitz Arabic two-hour tape to show him what I had been studying at home. I repeated, again like a parrot, the little everyday expressions I had picked up from the tape, such as greetings, buying a newspaper, ordering meals and drinks. He looked over his heavy-rimmed glasses and said, "Room for improvement, I think."

I was impressed with my first lesson, which I recorded on my minuscule cassette player.

The secret of absorbing a language into your brain is for the mind and the body to be physically tired. I find that the mind is more receptive late at night before going to sleep because the tiredness relaxes any nervous tension, and retention will be easier to absorb the words or phrases you have just learnt. So before sleeping, I would play my cassette for just ten minutes, and when I woke up the next day, I would repeat this process, repeating out loud along with the tape or cassette. This is a procedure which, over the years, I have found advantageous and a good method of mixing fatigue at night with retention of language the following morning.

This all took place eleven years ago, and since that first lesson, I have returned every year for five weeks to continue my studies with Wahid. In 2015, I was getting ready for my lesson and was watching the Tunisian news on television. I heard the shocking news that there had been a terrorist attack on a beach in Sousse, and thirty-nine people, mostly British, had been murdered. At the time,

Barbara and I were on a beach not too many miles from this atrocious act of wanton mass murder. This tragic incident did so much harm to tourism and the economy, and you cannot blame people for avoiding this country, fearing it could happen again. It completely tarnishes the image and reputation of this beautiful country with such kind and considerate people.

Eleven years spent with my teacher Wahid brought me the final accolade when the school presented me with my "certificate of excellence" *"en langue Arabe"*. I do hope that tourism will take off again so that people who have not visited the country will make their way to Tunisia and see for themselves how welcoming the people are. My mind again goes back to the Swiss lady we met in Egypt who denigrated all the Tunisian men she and her daughters encountered during their visit. It was thanks to her and her comments that I discovered this fascinating country.

*　　　*　　　*　　　*

Many years ago, I published a cookery book entitled, *A Cook's Tour of France*. We had a reception in the bar of our hotel the evening before the official book launch at the Hotel de France the next day. A guest staying in my hotel asked if he could speak to me about the overall running of the hotel and, in particular, the kitchen and the food produced in it.

"What is the secret of your success?" he asked.

I know that he was shocked by my response. I can still see the startled look on his face.

"I have done nearly everything wrong in the kitchen," I replied.

"You must be joking. What do you mean? I love your food. That's why I'm here!"

"Let me explain. For instance, when I put roast beef on the menu or roast lamb, I deliberately leave the joints in the oven for approximately forty minutes longer than I should. This is because my average guest is not accustomed to eating meat that has been perfectly sealed and still retains a pink texture in the centre.

"But that's how I like my meat cooked—well done and no blood," he replied.

"If the joint is well sealed, it will be pink in the middle, and there will not be any blood visible," I replied.

"Anything else?" he enquired.

"Well, yes, there is. Apart from meat and the way it is cooked, there is also the gravy. You must remember that the basis of a rich gravy comes from a reduction of beef bones, onions, carrot, leek and celery mixed with a residue left in the roasting dish to make what is known as a *'jus'* or *'les fonds de cuisine'*. This is the natural and very light gravy, but unfortunately, I have to thicken it with flour to make it extra thick or as some guests would prefer a product like Bisto. I am here to give people what they want and not to educate them."

I went on to explain – as I did earlier in this book – that one day, I served roast lamb beautifully sealed and pink in the centre. Mark was serving drinks to one of the tables when he heard one man say the following to his companion, "If the chef had taken this joint out of the oven half an hour earlier, we could have got this sheep back on its feet again." I then told the man the problem I have with vegetables. If I served them in the correct way, my guests would not eat them. Brussels sprouts, carrots and cauliflower need only a minimum of cooking in boiling, salted water, then drained to allow them to steam without any liquid, and then you add a large knob of butter, a squeeze of lemon juice and seasoning. So instead of serving *'al dente'* vegetables, I have to overcook them by about 10 minutes.

In the summer we always had a day when we served a cold table. That was when I could serve my home-cooked ham, which I cooked in a cloth, tied with string which held in the rosemary, Provence herbs, bay leaf and other flavourings. I would separately make my home-made mayonnaise, which is made with egg yolks, Dijon mustard, wine vinegar, vegetable oil, pepper, salt and a crushed clove of garlic (optional). Yet people would still ask for Hellman's mayonnaise.

"But that is what I like," the guest replied, "but Kraft, I think, is even better".

I then continued explaining that our sweet trolley always contained a varied selection of desserts and always a bowl of fresh fruit. On several occasions, a guest would ask if they could be served with tinned peaches or apricots as they did not like fresh fruit. So, to keep my guests happy, I have been obliged to do things differently to encourage them to return every year.

Food and languages have always been the two foremost elements in my life. In fact, one is synonymous with the other. If you see a simple word like cassoulet, you automatically think of the French language, pasta with Italian, Wienerschnitzel with German, paella with Spanish, couscous with Arabic, rice with Chinese. English, being the international language commercially and on the net, can at times be disadvantageous to the aspirations of people trying to learn a foreign language. How often, in France and Spain, have I heard the hackneyed expression of indifference to language learning with a sentence like, "Everybody here speaks English, what's the point of learning another language?"

A classic outburst I once heard in Torremolinos was after someone suggested going to an excellent restaurant and the person who was inviting his friends for a birthday celebration came out with the following sentence: "No point in going there—they only speak Spanish".

Over the years, I think I have stopped in nearly every village in France. Often when my car was parked outside a bar or restaurant, invariably, English residents living in France would make themselves known to me. Perhaps missing a bit of Old Blighty. They would come and sit with me, have a drink and talk about where they lived in the UK, what they did for a living and explain their reasons for living in France. But when the waiter came and spoke French to them, they had just one response: *"Je ne comprends pas"*. I have rarely come across British people, residing, in some cases twenty years or more in France, who can genuinely hold a conversation in French without fumbling in mid-sentence and saying, "Well, I can get by; they know what I mean". I think that, if one spends a certain amount of time in any country, then it is a mark of respect for its people and its culture to at least make some effort to socialise with the people and speak their language.

I also know that if one cannot speak one's own language correctly, it will certainly be an extra burden to speak another language fluently. At the moment, the beautiful English language, thanks to television and trendy broadcasters, has reached a new level of unfavourable smart phrases that have demoted standard English into an abyss of unrecognisable smart talk. I recently listened to all the television news channels, and this is what I heard.

"The Parliamentary session kicks off next week." It is not a damn football match. The following shows how word meanings have changed. I have put the correct English first—'We must face up to our enemy' now becomes 'We must face down our enemy'.

We must face up to the challenge = We must step up to the plate.

We must take time off = We must take time out.

I am in agreement with you = We are on the same page.

Repercussions = Blowbacks.

Escalator = Travelator.

Conveyor belt = Carousel.

Expand the economy = Grow the economy.

An Increase = Hike.

A big thing to ask = A big ask.

No progress = flatline.

Bring me up to date=bring me up to speed.

I know what you are getting at = I know where you are coming from.

He sneaked out of the room = He snuck out the room.

To increase production = to ramp up.

A detailed plan = Roadmap.

I need more time to myself = I need more me time.

I think I am now getting old and grumpy! I sympathise with foreign people wishing to speak our language when some of our leading and former politicians make the following mistakes. A perfect example of bad English is the following from educated people who should know better. The Prime Minister of the day, Mr Blair said in Parliament, in answer to a question from the Opposition leader at the time, Mr Howard, who asked, "Will the Prime Minister have the courage to make a statement to the House at Question Time?" His response was, "Yes, I will be stood there..." and in a different Parliamentary session, said, "Yes, last week when I was sat there..." And to commit more grammatical and verbal errors he said... "and the Home Secretary that I have appointed..." (should be whom). I find it quite disgraceful that in Parliament, not one person amongst approximately 650 Members had the courage to shout, "Prime Minister, speak English correctly!"

A few months ago, I received a letter from Buckingham Palace. It was in fact in reply to a letter I had sent just a few days before to Her Majesty the Queen telling her of my admiration for the manner in which she speaks. I pointed out that I heard her grandson, a future king addressing a large audience of students and he said the following... "All of you sat there..." and a day later at Sandhurst addressing the passing out of officers, said, "All of you stood there…"

RESIDENTIAL RESTAURANT LICENCE

The Mornington Hotel Limited

DON ROAD • ST. HELIER • JERSEY • JE2 4QD • CHANNEL ISLANDS

Proprietor & Managing Director: Mr. G. H. Anderson, A.I.L.
Telephone: 01534 - 724452   Facsimile: 01534 - 734131
Email: morningtonhotel@jerseymail.co.uk

1st February 2019.

Her Majesty the Queen,
Buckingham Palace,
London,
SW1A 1AA

Your Majesty,
    I have always been an ardent admirer of your command of the beautiful English language but the other evening I was horrified on hearing a speech by Prince William, who started with the sentence "All of you sat there …." obviously it should be all of you sitting there. This morning I was made aware of another speech he made at Sandhurst starting with the phrase "Indeed, it is no accident that you are stood here today …." Of course it should be "all of you who are standing here today."
    I sincerely believe that the heir to the Throne, who has received the very best of education should really follow your example and speak the Queen's English. This would not just be instructive for the benefit of the young, for whom the Prince is a role model but a continuity that your Majesty has set over the years.
    I remain,
        Your obedient Servant. Graham H. Anderson.

I simply find this bad and incorrect English unacceptable so I wrote in my letter that with the superior private education received by the future king, he should be setting a higher standard to students of his own and future generations. I think it was extremely courteous of Buckingham Palace to respond by return post. It just shows that someone still cares about the English language. As punishment for criticising the young prince, I can safely report, so far, that I have not as yet been sent to The Tower!

BUCKINGHAM PALACE

6th February, 2019

Dear Mr Anderson,

I am writing to thank you for your letter of 1st February to The Queen from which careful note has been taken of the views you express regarding a speech given by The Duke of Sussex recently.

I am forwarding your letter to the Office of His Royal Highness so your comments may be known.

Yours sincerely,

Miss Jennie Vine, MVO
Deputy Correspondence Coordinator

Mr Graham Anderson.

Recently, I went to have a coffee in a nearby Jersey tavern. A customer came in to order a pint and said that, because it was sunny, he would be outside on the terrace. The barman said, "Where will you be sat?" The customer replied, "I will be sat outside in the sun." I rest my case!

*   *   *   *

Away with politics and back to food. Confession, it is said, is good for the soul and liberates the conscience of guilt. We have known Christian and Régine now for some thirty years, and they have stayed with us nearly every year. Christian was the manager of the luxurious Hotel Malherbe in Caen. I always tried to impress him and Régine with original, creative dishes. Even though the hotel was closed, they came to visit us in the winter months. The last time they came, he had to remind me that I had promised to cook *'faux-filet aux truffes'* – sirloin steak with truffles – the last time we were with him in France. I didn't exactly panic because I like to keep my promises always. The fact that I did not have any truffles did not impede me in finding a solution to this problem. Could I get away with it? Yes, of course I did. I looked at the back of my fridge for a tube of truffle juice that I had bought in Périgueux. Next to this was a jar of Italian black olives. I cut and grated the olives as if I were preparing truffles and soaked the little strips in the truffle juice. I then sealed the steaks in my skillet pan with a small amount of oil, seasoned both sides and added a knob of butter. I took out the steaks and kept them warm. I then poured truffle juice into the pan and reduced it slightly. Then I added the four finely chopped black olives to the pan, and they looked just like truffles. Christian said it must have cost a fortune with so many 'truffles' in the sauce. Seriously he was so complimentary about the 'truffles' he and Régine ate, but this is the very first time that I have revealed this deception and misnomer of this classic French dish. Please forgive me, Christian and Régine, should you ever read my confession.

Two years ago, I celebrated a very special birthday. The rendezvous took place in St Malo. It had to be because I cannot explain the reason why but I never drink alcohol in Jersey, but I certainly do whenever I leave our beautiful island, so obviously a special birthday deserves a nice glass or two of wine. All the sons turned up with their loved ones at Café de l'Ouest, a famous fish restaurant in St Malo, along with other family members. The play on words started with the fish course…

Philip said, "This is the best plaice to have your party, Dad."

Lyndon said, "Oh my cod—the whiting's on the wall."

Alan interrupted, "Could you speak up, Dad? I'm hard of herring."

Jonathan said, "We are having a whale of a time."

I said, "You are all so quiet; what's the mackerel with you all?"

Then someone said, "I cannot take any more—I've haddock enough."

I said, "Just seeing you here makes my heart hake. I'd better get my skates on before I clam up and mussel in on other jokes!"

Finally, the last play on fish words has to be in French, so the reader who cannot work it out will have to try harder!

Hier soir j'ai mangé une aile de raie sur l'île de Ré!

Last night I ate a skate wing on the Island of Ré.

Hier soir, j'ai dormi comme un loir sur la Loire.

Last night I slept like a log on the Loire.

As we were finishing our meal, a Frenchman came up to me politely to ask my age. I said I always avoid this question by saying the following. "I was ten years younger than Roger Moore, and then he died, then I was five years younger than Omar Sharif, and then he died, then I was seven years younger than Sean Connery, and then he died—I am now looking for more candidates! How old are you, Sir?"

He shook my hand, smiled and went back to his table.

About the Artist

Lorand Sipos is a Hungarian artist based in Baja. He studied at the Hungarian Academy of Fine Arts in Budapest. He presently works for a cultural newspaper based in Baja. Lorand is a member of The Association of Hungarian Fine Artists.

His art works are represented in private gallery collections in Hungary, USA, Denmark, Germany, Sweden, Norway, Finland, Ireland, France, Croatia, China, Dubai, Canada, Australia, Transylvania and the UK.

Lorand says: In my works I try to portray the atmosphere around me in this new century. In our Complex world I need to find an artistic language that can translate my vision of the mingling of cultures and emotions. For me painting is a way of living, of expressing myself and my opinions, and I never cease to question and judge it.

About abstracts: If we pay attention to ourselves, listen to our inner voices, we notice our inner life, that our inner world is full of things, our self-knowledge. Our lives, inner- selves are abstract and deep.

How to tell a friend, how a concert was? How was an exhibition? Have we got words for abstract feelings, thoughts which appear in the moment?

The questions are how to express the unsaid, the feelings, the thoughts, the unformulated. These are the questions which I ask myself day after day, and as an artist I try to give answers with my art.

https://www.facebook.com/sipos.lorand

https://www.saatchiart.com/lorandsipos